Bible Study Series

D1504128

Revelation

Vision of Hope and Promise
Part 1

Marie Coody
Linda Shaw
Helen Silvey
Jeannie McCullough, Executive Editor

BEACON HILL PRESS
OF KANSAS CITY
KANSAS CITY, MISSOURI

Copyright 2000
by Beacon Hill Press of Kansas City

ISBN 083-411-7924

Printed in the United States of America

Cover Design: Darlene Filley

Library of Congress Cataloging-in-Publication Data

Coody, Marie, 1925-
   Revelation : vision of hope and promise / Marie Coody, Linda Shaw, Helen Silvey.
     p. cm. — (Wisdom of the Word Bible study series ; 3)
   ISBN 0-8341-1792-4 (pb)
    1. Bible. N.T. Revelation—Textbooks. I. Shaw, Linda, 1951- II. Silvey, Helen, 1931- III. Title. IV. Series.
  BS2825.5 .C66 2000
  228'.0071—dc21

                                                         00-039850

10   9   8   7   6   5   4   3   2

Contents

About Wisdom of the Word   4

Introduction to Revelation   5

L E S S O N   1   7

L E S S O N   2   15

L E S S O N   3   23

L E S S O N   4   31

L E S S O N   5   39

L E S S O N   6   47

L E S S O N   7   55

L E S S O N   8   63

L E S S O N   9   71

L E S S O N   1 0   79

L E S S O N   1 1   87

Notes   95

About Wisdom of the Word

Wisdom of the Word (W.O.W.) was founded in 1986 by Jeannie McCullough in Bethany, Oklahoma. It began as a weekly Bible study at Bethany First Church of the Nazarene. In the first year the study grew to over 400 members, and women from other churches and the community began joining. The local enrollment of Wisdom of the Word eventually exceeded 1,000 and has included men, women, and children of all ages and many denominations. Wisdom of the Word has been an instrument in uniting the community of believers as well as reaching the unchurched and the lost. It is now ministering to thousands through videos and cassette tapes and other programs such as Children of the Word, prison ministries, and missions.

About the Name

W.O.W. began as "Women of the Word." Then when men began to join in the study with the women, the name was changed to Wisdom of the Word, not only to retain the W.O.W. acronym but also to reflect the mission:

> To have our lives visibly changed by gaining wisdom from God's Word and responding in radical obedience to His voice.

About Jeannie McCullough

Jeannie McCullough is a pastor's wife, mother, and grandmother. Her life and ministry have taken her to Bethany, Oklahoma, where her husband, Mel, is the senior pastor at Bethany First Church of the Nazarene. She understands firsthand how radical obedience to God's Word can change a life.

Southern Nazarene University granted Jeannie an honorary doctorate in 1997. Due to her humor and honesty as well as her unique insights and application of the Scriptures in daily living, she is in great demand as a speaker throughout North America. Jeannie strives to be a "salt tablet" who will make others thirsty for God's Word. As she has committed herself to being a student of the Word, God has given her many opportunities to share what He is teaching her.

About the Authors

This is the third study presented by Wisdom of the Word. A team of three writers joined together to write lessons for this particular study:

• LINDA SHAW was the solo writer for the first W.O.W. study book on the Book of Ezra. She is the mother of Jonathan, Jenny, and Daniel. Linda is a licensed clinical social worker and began the W.O.W. prison ministry at a women's prison in the Oklahoma City area.

• MARIE COODY has been an integral part of the W.O.W. study since its beginning in 1986. She and her husband, Darwyn, have two grown daughters and are enjoying retirement.

• HELEN SILVEY is from a family of writers. She is a widow with four grown children. Helen has been a group leader for W.O.W. for many years and is very active in the life of Bethany First Church of the Nazarene.

Interested in starting a W.O.W. Bible study?

If you are interested in starting a W.O.W. Bible study, attending a study in your area, or ordering additional materials, please contact the W.O.W. outreach office in Bethany, Oklahoma, at 405-491-6274.

Introduction to Revelation

The Book of Revelation, *the revelation of Jesus Christ* (1:1), was written by John to the seven churches in Asia (modern-day Turkey) by John (verses 4, 9). Some controversy has arisen concerning the identity of John, but he probably was the beloved apostle, son of Zebedee and brother of James. The Early Church fathers almost unanimously agreed that he was the author, and tradition throughout history has affirmed this belief. The language and the many allusions to the Old Testament make it almost certain that the author was a Palestinian Jew writing in Greek but thinking in Hebrew, steeped in Temple and synagogue ritual, and very familiar with the Old Testament.

While John was in exile on the Isle of Patmos for preaching the gospel of Christ, he was told to write in a book the things he was to see in a vision, and to send it to the seven churches. Bible scholars disagree over the date Revelation was written, but most believe it was between A.D. 90 and 95.

The emperor of the Roman world at that time was Domitian, who demanded public worship of himself as lord and god. Prior to this, Christians had suffered persecution under Rome but mostly had been considered as a sect of seditious Jews, and much of the persecution had been at the hands of the synagogue and priests. Now Christians were confronted with a choice: Caesar (Domitian) or Christ. Once a year, everyone in the empire had to appear before the magistrates, burn incense to Caesar, and say, "Caesar is Lord." To address him in speech or writing required one to begin, "Lord and God." Refusing to call Domitian "Lord" and give him worship was considered an act of political disloyalty. The refusal of Christians to obey resulted in the second great wave of persecution against the Church. Christians were subjected to public ridicule, economic boycott, imprisonment, exile, even death. Revelation was written to comfort and strengthen them.

The Book of Revelation gets its name from the Greek word "apocalypse," which is translated "revelation" and literally means "an unveiling"—taking away that which obscures. Apocalyptic literature is a recognized style most common to the time between the Old and New Testaments but also frequently found in the Old Testament and in the first century A.D. It is called apocalyptic because it reveals truth expressed in symbolic and guarded language. Revelation is a Christian apocalypse, and its meanings were meant to be understood by these first-century congregations. The symbolism found in Revelation would have been very familiar to a people acquainted with Old Testament and apocalyptic writings.

The primary purpose of apocalyptic literature was to reveal the mysteries of God to believers experiencing oppression and suffering and to reassure them that despite the evil in this world, God will be the final Victor. A glimpse is given of the rewards of eternal life in heaven for all who overcome and remain faithful. Dark pessimism might be the theme on one page, only to be followed on the next page by a sudden, glorious breakthrough of God's power and might. This style of writing with its sharp, bold contrasts, drawing upon familiar symbols to speak about spiritual realities, was familiar to the people of the first century. Symbols are important as a way of understanding something difficult to explain or draw in a picture. One example is found in Revelation 17:5-6. Evil is difficult to explain, but *THE MOTHER OF HARLOTS AND OF THE ABOMINATIONS OF THE EARTH . . . drunk with the blood of the saints* paints with words a graphic description.

As you begin each day, use this acrostic to help you study:

Wait *for the Holy Spirit to teach you as you read His Word.*

Obey *what God instructs you to do.*

Remember *to praise God for insights and promises fulfilled.*

Discover *for yourself the incredible faithfulness of God!*

Revelation is also prophecy (1:3; 22:7, 18-19). Prophetic writing is even more common in Jewish and Christian literature than in apocalyptic literature. Prophecy contains an evangelistic and ethical message that intends to call people to repentance. Its meaning is not as mysterious or hidden as the apocalyptic; it has clarity and immediacy. It affirms God's will to us here and now with a cutting edge. It emphasizes our freedom in making decisions before God. It also predicts future events.

The use of numbers is very pronounced in Revelation, with 1, 3, 4, 7, and 12 being the favorites. The number 7 was used more than 50 times. Seven is the number of perfection, indicating completion and showing all things are accomplished according to God's plan.

Revelation is not plural; it is singular—one revealing vision. This revelation came from God, through Jesus Christ, to the angel, to John, to the churches, and to us. It deals with problems in seven first-century churches, problems representative of the Church in every age, everywhere. The *Expositor's Bible Commentary* refers to Revelation as a "unique source of Christian teaching and one of timeless reverence" and as the "most profound and moving teaching on Christian doctrine and discipleship found anywhere in Holy Scripture."[1] Through Revelation, God seeks to lead us into authentic Christian discipleship by explaining Christian suffering in the light of how Jesus' death bought us victory over evil, and telling us of the ultimate end of evil and final victory of the Lamb of God and His followers. The language of Revelation describes the reality of the conflict between the sovereignty of Christ and the satanic power of which Paul warns us in Ephesians 6:12.

Revelation is about many things—power, battles, freedom, faith, evil, hope, and warnings—but it has one great theme: Jesus Christ, the Son of Man in the midst of the churches in this present age, Judge and King in the dispensation to come, and the Lamb rejected yet someday to reign in glory on the throne, no longer meek and humble but with absolute power and control. The Gospels tell of Christ in His humiliation and death; Revelation reveals Christ in His majesty and glory.

Revelation also has a strong emphasis on worship, both on earth and in heaven. It also begins and ends with a special promise of blessing for obedient readers (1:3; 22:7), and it ends with a warning and curse for those who would tamper with it in any way (22:18-19).

This letter to the churches gives pastoral advice and spiritual counsel to help them resolve the problems threatening them spiritually. It is the written substitute for the work of a pastor. It seeks to define the presence and active participation of a good and sovereign Lord God in the midst of persecution, human misery, and social injustice. It was written for real believers struggling with real problems that threaten their faith. It is a call for repentance for the life and faith of every congregation of every age. Crises confront every generation of believers forming a community of faith who bear witness for God in a secular and materialistic world and face the temptation to compromise. And it reminds us that God rules above the ages and will accomplish His purpose in this age and the age to come.

Revelation is a difficult book but is definitely worth studying; you may learn to love it. If it is a hard book to understand, it is also a hard book to put down. Try not to begin your study of Revelation with preconceived ideas, but allow the Holy Spirit to teach you what God wants to say. Revelation is a book of warning, but for the faithful, obedient Christian, it is a book of glorious hope. Turn to Revelation when things seem darkest; God is in control, and "beyond the terror [is] the glory, and above the raging of men [is] the power of God."[2]

Written by Helen Silvey

Revelation

LESSON 1

■ **A Study of Revelation 1**

DAY ONE

Word of God

Read Revelation 1, concentrating on verses 1-3.

1. What is the main content of Revelation (verse 1)?

2. What are the two things to which John testifies?

3. In the Old Testament God promises us revelation. Read the following scriptures and tell what is to be revealed.

    Isaiah 56:1

    Daniel 2:28 and 47

4. John began each of his writings, which became books in the New Testament, with statements about how the Word of God was revealed in Jesus Christ. Summarize these scriptures.

    John 1:1

    1 John 1:1-2

    Revelation 1:1

5. We are also promised a future revelation beyond prophecies of the Old Testament and Jesus Christ in the flesh of the New Testament. Record the following passages that testify to this.

    Matthew 10:26

    2 Thessalonians 1:7

    1 Peter 1:13

6. From each of the following scriptures, give a phrase to describe the Word of God.

    Colossians 1:25-27

    Hebrews 4:12-13

MEMORY CHALLENGE

Psalm 103:1

*Bless the LORD, O my soul,
and all that is within me,
bless His holy name.*

7. According to Revelation 1:3, what are the three ways to be blessed?

In the Old Testament, each Hebrew book was named in accordance with its opening words. This is also true of Revelation, which is the revelation of or about Jesus Christ. One good definition of "revelation" would be "disclosure of fact." This book gives us a word picture of what will happen in the future, with Jesus Christ as the focus.

The process by which God makes known through visions the events of the final days on earth is called "apocalypticism." These are not dreams, but revelations of God. As we see in the Old Testament Book of Daniel, the revelation is generally brought by an angel to a seer as prophecy for the community of believers.

In Revelation 1:1 we are promised that this book is the divine disclosure of Jesus Christ. When He comes to claim His kingdom on earth, He will do so in power, glory, and triumph. Christ is the fulfillment once again of God's promises and His Word. *He is clothed with a robe dipped in blood, and His name is called The Word of God* (Revelation 19:13).

According to Revelation 1:3, the ones who read, hear, and heed the Word of God in the prophecy of Revelation are promised a blessing. Some commentators believe "read" means to read aloud in a group or worship service. Reading the Word of God is always a blessing. However, the Word must not simply be read, but must be heard in such a way that it causes us to obey or heed. James 1:23-24 tells us, *If anyone is a hearer of the word and not a doer, he is like a man who looks at his natural face in a mirror; for once he has looked at himself and gone away, he has immediately forgotten what kind of person he was.*

In the Greek language "blessed" means "happy," but in Hebrew it means bowing down before God and finding the right pathway amid many false pathways. It would mean the discovery of meaning and significance in the face of chaos or confusion. This was true of the Psalms and Proverbs, which often speak of our paths holding difficulties, problems, doubts, and hardships. But in spite of our circumstances, we can put our trust in Almighty God, who has everything under control and whose Word is always true.

C. S. Lewis wrote a wonderful series of stories for children titled The Chronicles of Narnia. One of the books, *The Horse and His Boy,* is the story of a young man named Shasta who is to warn the king of Narnia about an upcoming attack by the Tashians. His horse, Bree, is a wonderful aid to him, but on one nighttime occasion, Shasta has to ride a different horse, and the mountain path is treacherous. The horse refuses to obey his commands, and Shasta is overcome with fear. He begins to feel a presence beside him, although he can see nothing. When he attempts to learn the identity of the presence, the reply is simply "Tell me your sorrows." So Shasta complains that he is cold, tired, and hungry and that the task given him is too difficult. He laments about the long and dangerous journey, how lions have chased him, and that his childhood was unhappy. The answer given by the presence, who is Aslan the lion and the symbolic representation of Jesus Christ in C. S. Lewis's stories, is "I do not call you unfortunate." Why? Shasta is enduring hardship, but he is blessed, for he is on the correct path. He has Aslan beside him to comfort and guide him, as well as the promise of reaching his destination. Aslan never guaranteed Shasta that the assignment would be easy. He simply promised that if he stayed on the right road, he would accomplish it and, in the process, be blessed.

So blessed is the person who discerns the right path or the will of God and therefore derives the meaning of life in this way. Undoubtedly, the right road is the Word of God. *Your word is a lamp to my feet and a light to my path* (Psalm 119:105). As we study His Word in Revelation and choose to hear and heed, we, too, will be blessed.

Witness

Read Revelation 1:4-6.

1. If we understood Revelation 1:4-6 as describing the Trinity, which verses would describe whom?

   Father:

   Son:

   Holy Spirit:

2. Christ is described in three functions in verse 5. List these, and match them to the appropriate scripture.

   a.   Colossians 1:18

   b.   Psalm 89:27

   c.   John 8:18

3. List the three things Christ has done for us as described in Revelation 1:5-6.

4. Give a title to the five things Christ witnessed to in His ministry by filling in the blank for each of the following scriptures.

   Jesus witnessed to the

   Nature of _____   Ephesians 2:3

   Need for _____   2 Chronicles 12:6

   Nearness of _____   2 Peter 3:7

   News of _____   Luke 2:30[1]

5. Was this witness of Jesus always believed? Answer by summarizing John 3:11.

6. Jesus Christ bore witness of God's truth. Summarize the following scriptures.

   John 14:6

   John 18:37

7. God bore witness that He sent Christ. Summarize John 5:31-32, 37.

The Greek word for "witness" is translated "martyr," which could indicate verification or validation. Certainly a witness speaks from firsthand knowledge. This is what Jesus did, for He came to bear witness of the truth of God. In His witness, He revealed the name of God, the nature of sin and wrath, the need for righteousness, the nearness of judgment, and the news of salvation. Jesus Christ's witness was always and ever faithful to God.

These verses start with the typical greeting involving grace and peace, followed by an elaborate description of the Source of grace and peace, which includes the Trinity, a threefold description of Christ, and three characteristics of the salvation of Christ. This information is being sent to the seven churches in ancient Asia, which is not the same as present-day Asia. These seven churches basically represent all the good and bad churches throughout the ages. The churches are called to be a part of the kingdom of God, which in the New Testament is not territorial but a kingdom of relationship. *The time is fulfilled, and the kingdom of God is at hand; repent and believe in the gospel* (Mark 1:15). All believers are then called to be priests in the sense of offering spiritual sacrifices and praise to God. Revelation 1:4-5 refers to the fact that Jesus is known to individual believers. In verses 5-6, we see that Jesus is known to the Body of Christ. In verse 7, it is revealed that Jesus will be known to the world.

Matthew 24:14 tells us, *This gospel of the kingdom shall be preached in the whole world as a testimony to all the nations, and then the end will come.* Christ is the faithful witness, but we must remember that as we are to imitate Christ, we also are to become faithful witnesses. In this first chapter of Revelation, as His witnesses we are described as servants in verse 1 and blessed in verse 3. In verse 5 we're the beloved. In verse 5 we're also set free. Finally, in verse 6 we are commissioned to represent the kingship of God in the world as His priests and citizens. If we are faithful, we are promised that we will witness the return of the High King to establish His kingdom on earth.

What does being a faithful witness to Christ and God's kingdom mean to you? Are you taking seriously the fact that Christ will return to claim His rightful place as head of the kingdom of God on earth? Or are you living your life selfishly instead of witnessing of the truth of Christ to a sinful and dying world? At the close of this day's lesson, take several minutes to humble yourself before the Faithful Witness, and open your heart to what He may want to say to you.

In a Bible concordance or dictionary look up the word "bless," and define it here.

DAY THREE

Who Is, Who Was, Who Is to Come

Read Revelation 1:7-8.

1. What will happen when Christ comes with the clouds (verse 7)?

2. How does Christ describe himself in verse 8?

3. Throughout the Bible, God reveals himself and His Son through the term "I Am." Look up each of the following scriptures, and record the part that refers to "I Am."

   Exodus 3:6

   John 6:35

   John 8:12

   John 10:11

   John 11:25

   John 14:6

   John 15:5

   Revelation 21:6

4. What did God mean when He spoke of himself and His Son in verse 8 as *who is and who was and who is to come?* Write your own ideas, and then summarize the following scriptures.

   Psalm 90:2

   Hebrews 13:8

   Revelation 22:13

5. Our personal image of God is changed as we experience Him. Look up the following two stories, and write

who God became known as to His servants after they experienced Him.

Genesis 22:1-14

Exodus 17:8-16

6. Can you think of a way in which God became personal to you through experience? What name would you give Him to fit this situation?

In his book *Exploring Revelation,* John Phillips points out that the terms "Alpha" and "Omega" describe God in His omniscience. Omniscience is God's knowledge. God created everything and knows all there is to know about everything. He is also the beginning and the end, which means He is omnipresent. Omnipresence is the universal presence of God everywhere at all times from the beginning of time to the end of time. Finally, God is omnipotent. He has infinite power and is known as "the Almighty." In the *words who is and who was and who is to come,* we see the God of the past as revealed to us throughout His Word. We see Him in the present because we choose to believe. We see Him in the future because we have faith that what He has said and done in the past and present He will also do in the future.[1]

"Jehovah" is actually a compound word formed from three words. The first word means "He is," the second means "He was," and the third means "He will be" or "He will come." Another phrase that ties together "omniscience," "omnipresence," "omnipotence," and "Jehovah" would be "God is the Eternal."

Who is and who was and who is to come is a powerful tool for how God explains himself to humanity. His Word begins with *In the beginning God . . .* (Genesis 1:1) and then throughout the Bible gives us descriptions of Him in many ways and forms. One of the most graphic descriptions is His great "I Ams," of which *who is and who was and who is to come* is a form. For God to become personal to us, we must come to know Him in one of these "I Am" forms.

Becky was a single mother with two small children. She had a great faith in God and had seen Him lead her all the way through difficult days when her husband left her. Money was tight, but she just believed she should keep putting one foot in front of another and trust God for her needs.

One big problem for Becky was that she disliked her job. She thought the male boss was too friendly, while the other women in the office were catty and critical. The pay was only average, and a better-paying job would really help. She had to drive farther to work than she liked, and the company expected overtime when things were not finished—yet did not pay extra for it. She had no support system there, and each workday became a drudgery. She felt trapped because she needed the money the job provided.

One day Becky's boss called her into his office. He closed the door and became physically aggressive. By some miracle, she was able to get out of his grip, open the door, and flee. After she got home, she called the personnel department and resigned. She prayed, "Lord, I don't know how the kids and I are going to manage, but I'm at peace that this is what I'm to do."

The next morning as Becky got up for her devotional time of Bible reading and prayer, it came to her that God was her Deliverer. She felt led to read Psalm 144 and found in verse 2, *My lovingkindness and my fortress, my stronghold and my deliverer; my shield and He in whom I take refuge, who subdues my people under me.* That day God became even more personal to Becky because she came to know Him as her personal Deliverer.

When God delivered her, did He take care of her? Absolutely! During the next two months, the children's father was faithful to pay his child support. She received some money from her retirement account at her previous job and got an unexpected check from an unknown source. Her friends brought food, and her parents were able to pay her gas bill. Furthermore, she quickly landed a new job that was closer to home, paid better, never had overtime, and had two wonderful Christian women working there. Becky stayed at that job for eight years until she remarried and moved to another state.

When Becky waited on the Lord and refused to take matters into her own hands, she gave God an opportunity to be her Deliverer. But He also gave her an opportunity to know Him better through her own experience. He became even more personal. She knew Him as "I am your Deliverer." He is, He was, and He is to come. May we choose to experience those names too.

MEMORY CHALLENGE

Write Psalm 103:1 below.

DAY FOUR

Worship

Read Revelation 1:9-11.

1. In Revelation 1:9, John says that he is on the island of Patmos for two reasons that are titles of earlier days in this lesson. He was there because of the w_____ and Jesus Christ's _____.

2. Using a dictionary or Bible concordance, record a definition of "worship."

3. What happened to John when he was worshiping *in the Spirit?*

4. John must have prepared for worship. How do we prepare for worship? Give ideas from the following scriptures.

   Psalm 95:6

   Mark 12:30

   Acts 16:25

   Romans 12:1

   Hebrews 13:15

Patmos is one of the Sporades Islands and lies 37 miles west-southwest of Miletus in the Icarian Sea. John was banished there for about 18 months. He says he was a partner with fellow Christians in (1) suffering, to test and purify their loyalty, (2) the kingdom, and (3) faithful endurance. While isolated in this place, John developed his ability to worship. Willard Sperry emphasizes that "worship is a deliberate and disciplined adventure in reality."[1] John's worship was a daily discipline, and it certainly became an adventure.

Humanity is forbidden to give worship to any but God alone. This was originally lined out in the Ten Commandments and reiterated in Exodus 34:14: *You shall not worship any other god, for the LORD, whose name is Jealous, is a jealous God.* Jesus confronted Satan with this when He said, *It is written, "YOU SHALL WORSHIP THE LORD YOUR GOD AND SERVE HIM ONLY"* (Luke 4:8).

To be able to worship in the same Spirit as John did, we must certainly give our worship to God alone. This means not honoring anything or anyone above Him, but placing Him first on our priority list. We must never give more attention to our job, making money, helping the poor, raising our kids, or even working in the church. God must come first. As we put Him first, it becomes important in our daily lives to read His Word so we are familiar with all He has to say to us. Prayer is a priority as we learn to communicate with Him. Gathering as a body to lift up the name of the Lord in praise, singing, scripture reading, preaching, and prayer is vital. Putting aside our human activities so we can concentrate on God and His attributes opens an avenue into worship. When we worship, we are not only to praise His name but also to be ready like John to hear what God has to say to us. Part of worship is receiving what He has to give us.

So often we take worship for granted. To us it is "going to church." Do we go there each time to truly worship? Is being *in the Spirit* there most important to us, rather than what we wear, who we see, or how good the service is? What has caught your attention about worship in this lesson today? Challenge yourself to pursue that thought through prayer and more study or discussion with mature Christian friends. Find out for yourself what worship is and how God wants you to incorporate it in your life. Only through the discipline of doing this was John able to receive his revelation. God has something He wants to say to you too. Worship Him. Worship and be ready to receive.

MEMORY CHALLENGE

Fill in the blanks:

Bless the LORD, O my _____, and all that is

_____ me, _____ His holy name.

Psalm 103:1

DAY FIVE

Wow!

Read Revelation 1:12-17a.

1. What did John observe when he turned to *see the voice* that was speaking to him?

This revelation concerning the lampstand and the Son of Man was consistent with John's knowledge of the Old Testament. The lampstand is mentioned in Exodus 25:31, 37, as well as in Zechariah 4:1-2.

2. See how the following scriptures compare to the description of Christ in Revelation 1:14-16.

   Isaiah 49:2

   Ezekiel 8:2

   Ezekiel 43:2

   Daniel 7:9

   Daniel 10:5

3. Had John ever experienced such a thing in person? Learn about this or review it by summarizing Matthew 17:1-8.

4. What did John do when he saw the Son of Man?

What does this all mean? The seven golden lampstands and the description of Christ are indicative of Christ's role as High Priest. These were the garments and one of the instruments of a high priest. In the original Greek text, this section starting with Revelation 1:12 is a long quotation that doesn't end until 3:22. The seven golden lampstands are explained in 1:20, where we're told that they represent the seven churches, which are named in chapters 2 and 3.

The symbolism in this section is rich. The hair as white as wool and snow is a description from Daniel of the Ancient of Days. In Eastern countries white hair commands respect and indicates wisdom of years. It is also a symbol of purity.

Judgment is symbolized in several ways. The phrase *eyes . . . like a flame of fire* (verse 14) indicates the searching for righteousness or judgment. The *burnished bronze . . . glow[ing] in a furnace* (verse 15) represents judgment, since the instruments used for sin sacrifices in the Old Testament were made of this metal. The sharp two-edged sword that came out of His mouth is to strike the wicked: *From His mouth comes a sharp sword, so that with it He may strike down the nations* (19:15).

His voice, which was *like the sound of many waters* (verse 15), represented the majesty and glory of God. It's a description of God's own voice. His face, *like the sun shining in its strength* (verse 16), shows the glory of His countenance and His holiness.

Verse 20 describes Christ holding the seven stars in His hand. This is a sign of political authority and reminds us that the world and the church's ultimate fate is not in the hands of government or humanity but in the hands of God the Father and His Son, Jesus Christ. His right hand is a place of power and safety. Praise His name!

This description of Christ is important to us because it teaches us about His character and attributes. He is a reflection of the Father. As Christians, we want to know God the Father and His Son, Jesus Christ, in all their fullness. Wow! The revelation was overwhelming to John, but it's just as powerful in its magnitude to us. What an amazing God we serve!

MEMORY CHALLENGE

What does Psalm 103:1 mean to you spiritually?

DAY SIX

Write

Read Revelation 1:17b-20.

1. What were the first four words Christ spoke to John in his revelation?

2. John described how he saw Christ, but now Christ describes himself in the "I Am" form, as we studied in Day 3. Who does Christ say He is?

3. Record Revelation 1:19.

4. Use a dictionary to give a definition of "commission."

5. Read the following stories and summarize the commission God gave each of these persons.

   Judges 6:11-14

   Hosea 1:1-3

   Matthew 4:18-20

6. Using short phrases, summarize the requirements for a commission as described in the following verses.

   1 Samuel 3:9-10

   Matthew 26:39, 42

   2 Timothy 4:1-2

   2 Timothy 4:7

   1 Peter 3:13-14

7. Personalize 2 Timothy 2:15 as a summarization of what God expects in a commission.

Often a child of God who had a revelation first met it with fear. (For further study, see Ezekiel 1:28, Daniel 8:7, and Luke 1:26-30.) But immediately John is told, *Do not be afraid; I am the first and the last* (Revelation 1:17; see also Isaiah 44:6 and 48:12). Christ then states, *[I am] the living One* (Revelation 1:18). He has authority over death. While men killed Jesus, they did not know that death had no control over Him. When His time was completed, He became alive again. He states, *I have the keys of death and of Hades* (verse 18). The gates of death are referred to in several scriptures, including Psalm 9:13, 107:18, and Isaiah 38:10. But Christ proclaims that He has the keys. Keys give access to places. In the ancient world, the wearing of large keys was a mark of status in the community. To death and Hades, only one set of keys exists. Jesus Christ has them, and to Him we must come. *Because I live, you will live also* (John 14:19).

Christ commissioned John to write. He was to write of the past, present, and future. The past mainly refers to what John had already seen in his revelation. *The things which are* refer to the present state of the seven churches who are addressed in chapters 2 and 3. The future is described as *the things which will take place after these things* (verse 19) and comprises most of the rest of the Book of Revelation beginning with chapter 4. These chapters contain prophecy or events yet to occur in the future. How do we know they have not yet occurred? If they had, we wouldn't be here!

Twelve times in Revelation, John is told to write. It seems that God often affirmed His commission. Only once, in 10:4, is John told not to write.

When we are willing and ready and are listening to God, He will give us a commission too. We'll have to remain obedient and probably endure difficulties, but He'll empower us and give us the strength to persevere. Christ has a plan, a work for each of us to do. Henry Blackaby and Claude King in their study *Experiencing God* put it this way: "You cannot be in a relationship with Jesus and not be on a mission."[1] God has a commission for each of us.

God commissioned Jeannie McCullough many years ago to share with others what she had learned of Him in her walk. (See "About Wisdom of the Word.") This has led her to speaking with hundreds of people on airplanes as she travels, witnessing to salespeople in department stores, and stopping at strangers' houses to help with a simple chore in order to show the love of Christ. It has also led her to speak in numerous settings such as luncheons, retreats, and church services. Jeannie has been obedient to teach the Wisdom of the Word Bible study for 12 years. The study has literally reached thousands of people for Christ not only in salvation but also in rekindling a passion for God and developing a deeper relationship with Him. The commission has required willingness, endurance, and much listening. It has brought hardships, but also sweet rewards in doing the will and work of God.

Jeannie's commission has been to share the good news of Jesus Christ, and He has taught her personally. John's commission was to write. What is your commission? Do you know? If so, you're at a place of peace and contentment even in the midst of possible difficulties. If you're uncertain about your commission, be assured that God wants to make it as clear to you as He did to Jeannie and John. Stop now and take time to ask God where you stand in this area. Perhaps you lack willingness, readiness, or endurance. Ask God to show you the very point at which you need to begin to pray to discover your commission. John obeyed, and by doing so he preserved for us who live almost 2,000 years later the promise of our future with God. Because Jeannie obeyed and shared, God has changed hundreds of lives for the Kingdom. Our Heavenly Father has a special commission in mind for you. Pause now and pray. Let God speak to you.

Written by Linda Shaw

MEMORY CHALLENGE

Do you know the song that comes from Psalm 103:1? *Bless the LORD, O my soul, and all that is within me, bless His holy name.* Sing it to Him today, or, if you don't know it, recite it to Him as poetry.

Revelation

LESSON 2

■ A Study of Revelation 2

■ A Study of Revelation 2

DAY ONE

Our Local Church

Read Revelation 2, concentrating on the greetings to the churches in verses 1, 8, 12, and 18.

"Church" is the word used in the New Testament most frequently to describe a group of persons

    professing trust in Jesus Christ

    meeting together to worship Him

    seeking to enlist others to become His followers

God has given specific instructions directing believers on how to live as loving members of Christ's church.

Complete His instructions (using the *New American Standard Bible* if possible):

John 13:34-35	_____ one another.
Romans 12:5	We are . . . _____ one of another.
Romans 12:10a	Be _____ to one another.
Romans 12:10b	Give _____ to one another in _____.
Romans 12:15a	_____ with one another.
Romans 12:15b	_____ with one another.
Romans 12:16	Be of the _____ _____ toward one another.
Romans 14:13	Do not _____ one another.
Romans 15:7	_____ one another.
Romans 15:14	_____ one another.
Romans 16:16	_____ one another.
1 Corinthians 11:33	_____ for one another.
1 Corinthians 12:25	_____ for one another.
Galatians 5:13	_____ one another.
Galatians 6:2	_____ one another's _____.
Ephesians 4:32a	_____ _____ to one another.
Ephesians 4:32b	_____ each other.
Ephesians 5:21	Be _____ to one another.
Colossians 3:13	_____ with one another.
1 Thessalonians 5:11a	_____ one another.
1 Thessalonians 5:11b	_____ _____ one another.
Hebrews 10:24	_____ one another.
James 4:11	Do not _____ against one another.
James 5:9	Do not _____ . . . against one another.
James 5:16a	_____ _____ _____ to one another.
James 5:16b	_____ for one another.
1 Peter 4:9	Be _____ to one another.
1 Peter 4:10	Employ your special _____ in _____ one another.
1 Peter 5:5	Clothe yourselves with _____ toward one another.
1 John 1:7	Have _____ with one another.

Review these 30 scriptures, considering your obedience to each one. Obedience or disobedience are the only choices a believer has. Obedience is pure love for God; disobedience is the selfish desire to satisfy our own egos. As we study the seven churches John saw in his vision from God, we will understand how our disobedience to God's instructions weakens our local church.

DAY TWO

My Local Church

Read Revelation 2, concentrating on verses 2-3, 9, 13, 19.

In your own words, list the commendable qualities of these churches:

1. The church in Ephesus

2. The church in Smyrna

3. The church in Pergamum

4. The church in Thyatira

God loves these churches, but He loves them too much to leave them the way they are.

5. Record Luke 3:17.

The commendable qualities (the wheat) of these churches will live forever, but He is committed to burning up the chaff in their lives.

6. Summarize Matthew 22:37-40.

Obedience to these scriptures and those in yesterday's lesson is made possible when meaningful relationships have been established in a local body of believers with strong commitments to one another.

Oklahoma state senator Howard Hendrick was asked to speak to his local church during a fund-raising campaign for new buildings. His story reflects the "living out" of life in the local church:

I am excited about the new buildings our local church plans to build. But I am more excited about the journey it will take us on spiritually. Second Corinthians 9:6-8 says, *Now this I say, he who sows sparingly will also reap sparingly, and he who sows bountifully will also reap bountifully. Each one must do just as he has purposed in his heart, not grudgingly or under compulsion, for God loves a cheerful giver. And God is able to make all grace abound to you, so that always having all sufficiency in everything, you may have an abundance for every good deed.*

There are four kinds of people in our church:

1. There are those who have not given themselves to the Lord. They have not learned that all of the tithe is the Lord's. Malachi 3:8-10 says, *"Will a man rob God? Yet you are robbing Me! But you say, 'How have we robbed You?' In tithes and offerings. You are cursed with a curse, for you are robbing Me, the whole nation of you! Bring the whole tithe into the storehouse, so that there may be food in My house, and test Me now in this," says the LORD of hosts, "if I will not open for you the windows of heaven and pour out for you a blessing until it overflows."*

My experience has taught me that we cannot rob God. We end up with bills and other unexpected costs. Even if we could rob God, why would we?

2. There have been those who have been faithful with their tithes, but presently their financial means are relatively limited. God has opened up the windows of heaven with different blessings of talents or other spiritual gifts besides financial resources. I think especially of the widow in the story Jesus told. They are doing the best they can with the limited resources God has given them.

3. There is a group of persons who have been faithful with their tithes and from time to time have made additional offerings of a limited nature. The Bible says that without faith, it is impossible to please God. God is challenging these persons to please Him, with faith beyond obedience. God is teaching this group of people to trust Him by learning the joys of sacrificial giving.

4. The fourth group of persons are giving sacrificially already on a regular basis. They have learned the joy of sacrificial giving and have the faith to sow generously, and God is blessing them generously. They continue to sow generously again and again and again. In many cases these persons are giving more than half their income to various ministries to advance God's causes here and around the world.

I think of George Mueller, who prayed for all the funds necessary to fund dozens of orphanages in Britain. John Wesley said, "Make all you can, save all you can, and give all you can." Part of the capacity of these persons is that they have learned the value of sacrificial living. Part comes from their careful spending, part from their careful saving, and part from their careful investing. They have proven their worthiness as a steward with whom God can trust more and more resources.

Wherever we fit into these categories, God can teach us to grow.

When my wife, Tracy, and I prepared to reach a decision about what our part would be in giving to this building campaign, I was drawn to verse 7 of 2 Corinthians 9: *Each one must do just as he has purposed in his heart, not grudgingly or under compulsion, for God loves a cheerful giver.*

I remember years ago, in response to another plea for funds, I lacked the spiritual maturity to recognize that my commitment should not be made grudgingly nor under compulsion. I wasn't mature enough to listen to God only and not to my peers. I felt under compulsion. I fulfilled that commitment. It wasn't a very rewarding experience.

A lot of factors have gone into the decision Tracy and I have made about our commitment today. We have four children. Three of them are fairly young. We are committed to keeping Tracy at home while they are young. So we have only my income to meet our commitment. In addition to our children, we both have aging parents. While we hope our parents' resources will be adequate to meet their needs, the truth is that one never knows. We are concerned about our parents' care. Our oldest child is in high school, and we have the concern of adequately preparing for the resources that are necessary to save for her college education.

Our family time is crowded with softball games, soccer games, T-ball games, basketball games, Bible quizzing, Sunday dinners, birthday parties, band concerts, and trips to the vet with our Great Pyrenees.

And then there are the responsibilities to my clients as a lawyer, my responsibilities to many of you in the state senate, and a host of other boards and committees on which I serve.

I said all of this to say that our family is busy. My time is jammed. Our resources are stretched, but we have decided to trust God to fulfill a pledge that will stretch us farther than we have ever been stretched before. I can say, though, that this time we're not giving under compulsion. We are giving cheerfully.

I grew up about five blocks from here, so I love this place. I remember the groundbreaking for this sanctuary. I must have been 10 or 11 years old. It was in this place that Helen Silvey led a junior choir in which I sang. It was in this place that Forrest Ladd led a summer institute where I memorized a lot of scripture. It was in this place that Elmer Shellenberger, John Bumpus, and Marvin Griffin taught me to play ball. It was in this place that Hal Perkins and I played one-on-one in basketball, and after he wore me out, he shared his faith with me. It was in this place that I was baptized as a child. It was in this place that I came to

confess my sins—many, many acts of selfishness. God waited here for me lovingly, ready and generously willing to forgive me.

It was in this place I have been a best man, and I have also been a pallbearer. It was in this place that Tracy and I were married and Chelsea was dedicated, Callie was dedicated, Christiana was dedicated, and Hudson was dedicated. It was in this place I was baptized as an adult, recognizing I had strayed from the Lord from the time I was first baptized as a child, now better appreciating, though still learning, what it means to be crucified with Christ.

My friends have been memorialized here. I have laughed here. I have cried here. It is here I have been a slave to my sins, and it is here I have been set free from them. Most importantly, it is here I have personally experienced God's amazing grace.

It is not the address of this place that makes it special. It is He whom I have met here that has transformed my life. The warmest memories of my life have taken place here, and I can say with David, *I was glad when they said to me, "Let us go to the house of the LORD."*

Giving this money and building these buildings will be easy compared to the work of ministering to the needs in our neighborhood that will follow after these buildings are built. The world is full of empty monuments to architects built in the name of the Lord. If this place is to be a transforming center for the work of the Lord, we will have to pledge more than our money for its construction. We will have to pledge our time, our talents, our treasures, and our very lives to the Lord himself. We can give generously only because He has first given generously to us to give us the joy of returning it to Him. To Him alone be the glory, for He has cheerfully given to each of us the best that He could give, even the indescribable gift of the only Son He ever had. Praise His generous name!

Are you willing to make a sacrificial commitment as Senator Hendrick did? When you meet God face-to-face, are you confident that your level of commitment will allow Him to greet you with *Well done, good and faithful servant! . . . Come and share your master's happiness* (Matthew 25:21, NIV)?

MEMORY CHALLENGE

What are some of God's benefits?

DAY THREE

Ephesus:
Restore Your Love

Read Revelation 2:1-7.

1. How is Jesus Christ described in verse 1?

2. How does Revelation 1:20 interpret this description of Jesus Christ?

3. What caused great disappointment for Christ in the church at Ephesus?

4. In verse 5, what exhortation did Christ speak to the Ephesians?

5. What was to happen if they did not heed His instruction?

6. What promise did Christ give if they overcame their sin?

There is so much good in the church at Ephesus that it comes as a surprise to learn that they had left their first love. They were doing all the right things—but for the wrong reasons.

Psalm 139:1 tells us, *O LORD, You have searched me and known me.* Jesus knew the motives behind all their activities. He knows His Church and is deeply concerned for its well being. He sees what's good and what's bad, urging us to faithfulness and at the same time demanding repentance when we sin by choosing the love of spiritual activity before the love of serving the Lord.

The church at Ephesus had been established by Paul and his disciples during the missionary journeys in A.D. 53. In

A.D. 62 Paul wrote his Ephesian letter to encourage those believers. After Paul's death in Rome, Timothy, Apollos, and later John traveled to Ephesus to minister to the Ephesian church. In A.D. 95-96 the church at Ephesus needed the Lord's evaluation, because the church that had been salt was losing its saltiness, and the light of the church was being hidden under a bushel (see Matthew 5:13-16), a bushel of activity without love.

How can a church—or individual—recover from this? Revelation 2:5 tells us to remember, then repent, then do. Do we *remember the height from which [we] have fallen* (NIV) when we've lost our first love?

Take a look back. Remember what it was like when you first came to Jesus. Recall the joy you had in the Lord, the closeness you felt to Him and Him to you. Remember the inner support that was there in times of pressure and trouble, the ease with which you prayed. Remember the delight you took in other Christians, in the reading of the Word, and how you couldn't miss a service because you were learning so much truth about life.

Now repent. Change your mind. That's what repentance means. Change your mind about what has taken the place of Jesus in your life. Put the Lord back in the center of all of your endeavors. Repent.

Then do. *Do the deeds you did at first,* Jesus says (verse 5). What are those things you did at first?
- You read your Bible, longing to find out what the Word of God said.
- You prayed about everything—even finding a parking place. You responded to the hurts and the needs around you with compassion and love.
- You praised God from your heart continually. You loved to sing His praises and to think about His grace, mercy, and love to you.

Now do that again, Jesus says. Start there. *To him who overcomes, I will grant to eat of the tree of life which is in the Paradise of God* (verse 7). Our Lord is himself the tree of life. Feed upon the tree of life. Listen to what Jesus says, and obey Him, and you will soon find your spiritual life flourishing. You will grow strong in the pressures and struggles that come your way.

MEMORY CHALLENGE

What are the benefits you are personally experiencing from God?

Smyrna:
Faithful in Suffering

Read Revelation 2:8-11.

1. How is Jesus described in the following verses?

   Revelation 1:17-18

   Revelation 2:8

   Revelation 22:13

2. Record Isaiah 44:6.

The title "Him" who is the First and the Last was through the prophet Isaiah (44:6). It describes the sovereign and mighty God of Israel. Jesus Christ, the Son of God, informed the Church that He has the same title as His Father. All of creation, all of life—past, present, and future—is in the mind, heart, and hands of our Lord Jesus Christ. He is the only living God, the King of Israel, their Redeemer and life. Outside of God, revealed in Jesus, there is no other source of life, wholeness, joy, or peace. And He is alive forevermore!

3. What does Jesus know about the local church in Smyrna?

4. What instructions does He give the church?

5. How will martyrs be rewarded?

6. What promise is given to those who overcome the sufferings of the church in Smyrna?

The church of Smyrna, unlike the church of Ephesus, had not forsaken their first love but were prepared to suffer for their love of Jesus in a hostile community. The church was composed of poor people, with no comparison to the number or the prestige of the church of Ephesus. Many of them were Roman slaves or servants and lived in abject poverty. They became even poorer financially because of their bold witness for Jesus in the marketplace; the Jewish and pagan merchants would not trade with them. In spite of the stress of physical poverty, the Christians in the church of Smyrna were spiritually very rich in all the things that mattered to the heart of God. They were living examples of 2 Corinthians 8:9, which tells us, *You know the grace of our Lord Jesus Christ, that though He was rich, yet for your sake He became poor, so that you through His poverty might become rich.*

Smyrna was a coastal city of great wealth, located 40 miles north of Ephesus. It had a protected harbor on the western shore of Turkey, which permitted a flourishing trading business. Archaeologists have found evidence of first-century Jewish settlements there. Smyrna was also noted as a strong center for emperor worship. In 195 B.C. a temple to the goddess of Rome was constructed, and in A.D. 26 a temple to Tiberius was also constructed. These and other temples were built upon an acropolis that produced a very dramatic visual effect and was popularly described by the phrase "the Crown of Smyrna."

Smyrna was a city where learning, especially in medicine and the sciences, flourished.

With Smyrna being the first city chosen by Rome in which to build a temple to the emperor Tiberius, it was the heart of the sinister Caesar cult. To refuse to sprinkle incense on the fires before Caesar's image and declare him Lord, the living God, was interpreted as a lack of Roman patriotism and disruptive of the unity of the empire. The Christian community experienced financial, emotional, and spiritual suffering because of their loyalty to Jesus as Lord.

I know . . . the blasphemy by those who say they are Jews and are not, but are a synagogue of Satan (Revelation 2:9). Since the days when Jesus began His ministry on earth, the unbelieving leaders of the Jewish community had refused to accept Him as their Messiah. They were looking for a king to overthrow the Romans and set up his kingdom. Jesus came as a suffering servant. When He eventually was crucified for the sin of humanity, the Jewish leadership rejected Him again as their Messiah. When He was evaluating the church of Smyrna, Jesus looked at the hearts of the Jewish leadership and saw them not as a faithful remnant who were looking for their Messiah, but as a group of men ruled by Satan and meeting in a synagogue to make plans to destroy His flock. Jesus came to this earth to bring the gift of life, but they existed to bring death on the Christian community, all in the name of God.

The remnant of authentic believers in our own country will come under more stress and suffering because of our spiritual and moral stand against many of the current social issues that our government would call good and we would call evil in the sight of God. "Political correctness" is the watchword of the day rather than truth and righteousness as defined by Jesus Christ. Notice that Jesus gave no word of correction to the suffering church at Smyrna, because in their suffering they had drawn close to Him. But now He gave a loving exhortation, *Do not fear what you are about to suffer* (verse 10). This persecution was designed by Satan to destroy the Christians, but the Lord used it to test them, to purify their faith in Him as well as to reveal the genuine believers within the church.

He who overcomes will not be hurt by the second death (verse 11). All of us who have been born will physically die unless Jesus comes back first, all of us will experience a bodily resurrection unless He comes back first, and all of us will live forever—but not all of us will live in eternity with Jesus Christ. Those who reject Him as their Lord will experience the *second death*—eternal separation from God, alone and in torment.

Revelation 20:12-15:
> *And I saw the dead, the great and the small, standing before the throne, and books were opened; and another book was opened, which is the book of life; and the dead were judged from the things which were written in the books, according to their deeds.*
>
> *And the sea gave up the dead which were in it, and death and Hades gave up the dead which were in them; and they were judged, every one of them according to their deeds.*
>
> *Then death and Hades were thrown into the lake of fire. This is the second death, the lake of fire.*
>
> *And if anyone's name was not found written in the book of life, he was thrown into the lake of fire.*

These are difficult days for the Church of Jesus Christ around the world and now in the United States. We know that Jesus is giving Satan permission to test His Church at different times to purify it. The persecution may come from the government, irate citizens, or the religious community. How are we to react to this persecution? Stop being afraid, because Jesus is in full control of His Church, and the gates of hell will not overcome it. Remain faithful to Jesus Christ up to the point of death or until He comes again. Then He will give you the *crown of life.*

MEMORY CHALLENGE

Fill in the blanks:

Bless the Lord, _____ _____ _____, *and forget*

_____ *of His* _____.

Psalm 103:2

Pergamum:
Faithful in Temptation

Read Revelation 2:12-17.

1. How is Jesus described in the following verses?

    Revelation 1:16

    Revelation 2:12

    Revelation 19:15

Christ is introduced as the One who has the sharp sword with two edges. The sword refers to the Word of God. The Word of God by its promises and message of salvation cuts loose the chains of sin and condemnation that bind the helpless sinner. The same Word of God is the means of condemnation and rejection for those who refuse its message of grace and forgiveness. The Word of God is at once the instrument of salvation and the instrument of death—the double-edged sword.

2. What does Jesus know about the local church of Pergamum?

3. What faults has Jesus revealed to the church of Pergamum?

4. Record the strong warning Jesus gave.

5. What is promised to those who overcome the false teachings and evil practices of the local church of Pergamum?

The faithful church of Smyrna endured persecution, but the church of Pergamum was faced with the enticement of compromise and corruption. It was being undermined by corrupt practices and corrupt teaching. This church needed to hear the truth of God in the midst of the temptation to give in to heretical teachings that led to sexual immorality and idolatry. They then needed to repent before Satan destroyed their faithful witness.

Located about 50 miles north of Smyrna, Pergamum was the Roman capital of the province of Asia. It was the center of pagan worship, and a temple to Caesar was located there—described in verse 13 as *where Satan's throne is.*

Satan had set up his throne to rule Pergamum from the temples dedicated to the Roman Caesars. Their ceremonies forced true citizens to declare their loyalty to Rome by bending their knee to Caesar as lord. To have a group of Christians declare Jesus as Lord was a political threat of disloyalty to the government. But Christians were told by our Lord not to escape, but to remain as faithful witnesses. From this evil threat, a small group of Christians were seeking by the indwelling power of the Holy Spirit to remain faithful to Jesus.

We have no information about who Antipas was (verse 13), but some Christians were put to death in this city because they refused to sprinkle incense into the fire burning below the bust of Caesar and declare, "Caesar is Lord." They died because they declared publicly and privately that Jesus Christ was their personal Lord, Savior, King, and sovereign Lord, who had saved them from their sin and was willing to save all who turned to Him.

Christians today still face persecution in some parts of the world. Recently in Iran, three prominent Evangelical pastors were abducted and assassinated. Many Christians have been arrested and tortured; others have lost their homes, jobs, and businesses. All ethnic, Armenian, and Assyrian Christian schools have been closed or taken over by Muslims.

The teaching of Balaam (verse 14) corrupted and enticed Christians into the sin of sexual immorality. The counterpart we face today is the practice and addiction of pornography and fornication among Christians and the general acceptance of living together without marriage that is common even in churches today. The error of Balaam continues today.

[Holding to] the teaching of the Nicolaitans (verse 15) is harder to define. It is difficult to know exactly who these people were, but the name means "conquerors of the people." It appears they claimed to have a special relationship to God. They claimed to receive revelations that were not given to others; therefore, they were more knowledgeable of God. They presumed to take the place of the priesthood of Judaism and carried that error into the Christian church.

Probably both of these false teachings worked together. One appealed to physical lust and the other to the ambition for power exercised in a religious way. It is seen yet today in the supremacy of pastors who are lifted up above the laity and are regarded as better than the rest of the people. The way to handle either error is with the sharp two-edged sword. Jesus said, *Repent therefore! Otherwise, I will come to you and will fight against them with the sword of my mouth* (verse 16, NIV). The Word of God exposes both the error of immorality and the error of priestly or spiritual superiority. Jesus says in verse 17, *To him who overcomes, to him I will give some of the hidden manna.* In John 6:41 we learn that Jesus is the hidden manna, *I am the bread that came down out of heaven.* He is food for the inner spirit, food that others don't know about. In John 4 Jesus had sent the disciples into the city of Sychar to get food. When they came back, they found he had been ministering to the woman at the well. He told them, *I have food to eat that you do not know about* (verse 32). He was feeding upon the inner strength that God the Father was giving Him. That is what is given to those who resist the lure of immorality and spiritual privilege.

Then along with the hidden manna comes the white stone with a secret name upon it. White stones were used among the Romans as a mark of special favor and privilege. A secret name is a special mark of intimacy. If you know the Lord Jesus, and your heart is kept pure from the corrupting influences of the world, you will enjoy an intimacy with Him in which the new nature He has given you (depicted by the new name in this scripture) becomes stronger and more developed, and you will enter into beautiful fellowship and intimacy with Him.

Thank You, Father, for Your mercy and grace to us each day. Thank You for teaching us so plainly and clearly in these letters what we are to recognize and evaluate in our own lives. Help us, Lord, to heed what the Spirit says to the churches. We pray in Jesus' name. Amen.

MEMORY CHALLENGE

Write out Psalm 103:1-2.

Thyatira:
Holy Amid Compromise

Read Revelation 2:18-29.

Jesus, the Son of God, has *eyes like a flame of fire* (verse 18), eyes that can pierce the facades, the disguises, and the hypocritical lifestyles of His creation and get right to the heart of what they are doing. He has feet *like burnished bronze,* which can trample sin under foot and severely punish that which is wrong. Both were needed in the church of Thyatira. It was the most corrupt of the seven churches.

1. What does Jesus know about the church of Thyatira?

2. What faults did Jesus reveal to the church of Thyatira?

3. Record Revelation 2:21.

4. What strong warning did Jesus give?

5. What assurance does Jesus speak to the faithful members of the church?

6. What is promised to those who overcome and keep His deeds to the end?

There is no recorded history of the beginning of the church of Thyatira, but it appears that they had little if any governmental or religious pressure against them. The local trade guilds challenged the Christians' consciences, because membership involved a demanding social life, pagan rituals, and periodic feasts at which members ate meat offered to idols and participated in sexual orgies. At the same time, these Christians feared that if they left the guild it might cripple their social and business network. Then, as an additional pressure, the Christian workers were faced with a growing heresy within the church itself, which the elders refused to address.

But there were some good things going on in Thyatira. If you and I had been there, we would have been greatly impressed by this church. It was a busy, active congregation with some wonderful people in it who manifested good deeds, love and faith, concern and care for others, and they were growing spiritually in their relationship with the Lord.

You tolerate the woman Jezebel (verse 20)—what picture came to your mind when you read the name "Jezebel"? The Jezebel of the Old Testament ranks as the most evil woman in the Bible (1 Kings 16:28—2 Kings 9:37). She symbolizes people who totally reject God and promote their own gods, causing their followers to enter into idolatry and all the sexual immorality connected with their rites. The elders of the church of Thyatira were tolerating this self-appointed false prophetess by the same name, and her teachings.

The Lord had shown patience and mercy to Jezebel, hoping she would repent. She did not, so He saw that severe judgment needed to be given to her, her spiritual children (who were spreading her deadly theology within the church), and her followers. What a reminder to all of us, *I will give to each one of you according to your deeds* (verse 23)!

Today, as then, the result of judgment and discipline within the church is that the church is purified, strengthened, and helped. People begin to take note of evil tendencies and become careful not to drift into the pattern of worldly society. They are willing to stand against what is evil and, if necessary, take action to correct it. That's what needed to happen in Thyatira.

A time is coming when faithful believers will rule the nations with Jesus. We will have a place of privilege and responsibility. Evil nations will be shattered in that day. In Revelation 22:16, Jesus refers to himself as *the bright morning star.* Christians in Thyatira, who had rejected Jezebel and her teaching of darkness, would receive the Bright Morning Star, Christ himself, and in His power they would be able to be holy as He is holy—a promise to the Christians of Thyatira, a promise to us.

Written by Marie Coody

MEMORY CHALLENGE

Quote aloud Psalm 103:1-2.

Revelation

■ **A Study of Revelation 3**

DAY ONE

Fruitless Church

Read Revelation 3, concentrating on verses 1-3.

1. To whom was this first letter addressed? Do you believe it has relevance for us today? If so, how?

2. The New Testament frequently likens sin to death (verse 1). Record these verses:

   Romans 6:13

   Ephesians 2:4-5

3. In Revelation 3:2-3, we find five direct commands from the risen Christ. List them.

4. No commandment appears more frequently in the New Testament than *wake*, *watch*, and *be alert*. Summarize these verses:

   Matthew 24:42; Matthew 25:13; with Mark 13:32-33, 37

   1 Thessalonians 5:2

5. The author of Hebrews recorded this warning: *We must pay much closer attention to what we have heard, so that we do not drift away from it* (Hebrews 2:1; see also Revelation 3:3). Jesus spoke of those who have drifted away and are no longer spiritually alive and vital. Summarize His words in these verses:

   Matthew 5:13

   Matthew 24:12-13

   Mark 4:18-19

6. Read Luke 13:6-9. Explain what this parable says to you concerning a "fruitless" life for those professing to know Christ.

7. In addition to being alert and watchful, how are we to live until Christ returns? Use the following verses to help you with your answer.

John 15:5 with 1 John 2:28

1 Thessalonians 5:22-23

1 Timothy 6:14

I see right through your work. You have a reputation for vigor and zest, but you're dead, stone dead.

Up on your feet! Take a deep breath! Maybe there's life in you yet. But I wouldn't know it by looking at your busy-work; nothing of God's *work has been completed. Your condition is desperate. Think of the gift you once had in your hands, the Message you heard with your ears— grasp it again and turn back to God* (Revelation 3:1-3, TM). This is the accusation the Risen Christ makes against the church at Sardis.

Sardis was a leading city of Asia during the first century A.D. It was a city of immense wealth from gold, extensive fruit orchards, textile industries, especially fine woolens, and jewelry factories. Built on a steep hill at the junction of five roads connecting it to all of the Roman world, this supposedly impregnable city had been captured twice because of a lack of vigilance by its citizens. The luxurious living had led to immorality, and the peace of Roman rule (the Pax Romana) led to a lethargic atmosphere of living on past dreams of grandeur. Unfortunately, these conditions had also infected the church.

Many inhabitants of Sardis became Christians during the first century and established a church that was prosperous and led a comparatively sheltered existence. The result was yielding to the temptation to become slack and lifeless. It is likely that the Jews and Romans did not persecute this church, as they did the other churches, because of its lack of an aggressive and positive Christian witness. Why should Satan waste his time persecuting a church or a people who aren't aggressively living and witnessing for Christ? The church at Sardis was one with a reputation for being alive and relevant with an effective ministry. It may have pleased people, but it didn't please God! Christ looks not on outward appearance, but on the heart, and He proclaimed boldly that the church of Sardis was dead as far as spiritual life and power were concerned (see Luke 6:26).

A boy named Jimmy received a telescope from his parents for his birthday. Eagerly, he went with his father and the

new telescope to a dark area away from the city lights to view the night sky. The father explained that the light from a particular polar star takes 33 years to reach earth.

"Do you mean," asked Jimmy, "if that star went out 30 years ago, I could still see its light in the sky tonight?"

"Yes," answered the father. "You could still see its past light even if it was actually dead and dark now."

That was the condition of the church at Sardis, and sadly, it is true of many churches and Christians today. They are living on the reputation of their past, but they are dead and useless to God and His kingdom, full of activity and busy-ness, but with little spirituality and *holding to a form of godliness, although they have denied its power* (2 Timothy 3:5).

In his commentary on Revelation in *The Daily Study Bible Series*, William Barclay writes, "The church is in danger of death when it begins to worship its own past . . . when it is more concerned with forms than with life . . . when it loves systems more than it loves Jesus Christ . . . when it is more concerned with material than spiritual things."[1]

In this letter to the church, Christ gives us five commands that will revitalize our churches and our individual lives as well if we obey them:
1. Wake up!
2. Strengthen the positive things that still remain before they die.
3. Remember what you have received and heard.
4. Obey.
5. Repent.

Is your walk with Christ still vibrant and alive? Is your prayer life and time spent in the Word energizing and meaningful? If your walk with Christ has become dull and lifeless and merely routine, ask Christ now to help you strengthen the positive attributes still present in your Christian walk before they die. Remember His loving sacrifice for your salvation and the joy of His presence in your life. Become radically obedient. Ask His forgiveness for allowing other things to replace Him on the throne of your heart or permitting memories of past victories to replace a vital relationship with Him now.

Lord, help me to constantly abide in You, that my relationship with You might always be alive and vital, and that I might bear fruit and be useful for You.

Faithful Few

Read Revelation 3:4-6.

1. The risen Christ gives John three promises for those who have overcome and *have not soiled their garments.* List them.

2. Throughout the ages, white has signified purity. Record Psalm 51:7.

3. Read Isaiah 1:16. Have you been cleansed from all sin and unrighteousness and your sins made *whiter than snow* (verse 18)? Write out God's loving, merciful promise in 1 John 1:9.

4. Record 1 Thessalonians 4:7.

5. According to Hebrews 12:14, what is required of us to see the Lord?

6. Look up "sanctify" or "sanctification" in your dictionary, and write the definition. Do not discuss doctrinal differences regarding when or how sanctification is received.

7. Record 1 Thessalonians 5:23-24.

8. We are to come before God without blame. How should we serve God daily, according to Luke 1:74-75?

9. Mother Teresa once said, "We must live each day as if it were our last so that when God calls us, we are ready and prepared to die with a clean heart." Summarize Romans 12:1.

A ray of hope shines through the darkness in the church at Sardis. A few members have remained faithful in their walk with Christ and *have not soiled their garments.* According to Bible translator and commentator John Moffatt, in Asia Minor, where Sardis was located, "soiled clothing disqualified the worshipper and dishonored the god."[1] These few who have remained pure are worthy of the honor of being clothed in white and walking with Christ for eternity.

To come into God's presence with our thoughts and/or actions soiled by sin would dishonor Him. We must keep free from sin if we are to have fellowship with God (1 John 3:6). If your garments are soiled from sin, they can be washed in the blood of the Lamb and made white again. Ask God now for forgiveness and for the strength and power to live a life that will be pleasing to Him, your thoughts and actions guided by the Holy Spirit. We are able to be overcomers, not in our own strength or cleverness or ability, but only by the blood of the Lamb and the power of the Holy Spirit in our lives.

Not only will the overcomer be clothed in white, but the name of the overcomer will not be erased from the book of life. When the Israelites sinned against God by making and worshiping the golden calf, Moses asked God to forgive their sin or *blot me out from Your book* (Exodus 32:32). The Lord told Moses, *Whoever has sinned against Me, I will blot him out of My book* (verse 33). In Daniel 12:1 we learn that in the great distress of the end time, everyone whose name is in the book will be rescued. Only those whose names are in the Lamb's book of life will enter the New Jerusalem (Revelation 21:27). According to 20:15, those whose names are not found in the book of life will be thrown into the lake of fire. But Jesus says He will confess the names of the overcomers before His Father and the angels and will deny before His Heavenly Father those who deny Him before others (Matthew 10:32-33).

Are you listening carefully to *hear what the Spirit says to the churches* and to you? Do you confess Jesus as Savior and Lord? Is your name written in the Lamb's book of life? Are you living in faithful, radical obedience to Him?

Lord, may You always find me faithful.

Who pardons your iniquities and heals your diseases?

Faithful Church

Read Revelation 3:7-13, concentrating on verses 7-8.

1. How did the angel of the church in Philadelphia describe Christ?

2. Christ put an open door before this church. According to verse 8, why can no one shut this door?

3. Jesus has the key of David. Record Isaiah 22:22.

God gave Isaiah this message concerning His servant Eliakim (Isaiah 22:20), who would become King Hezekiah's faithful steward and would be given the key to all the treasures of the king; only he could open or shut the door. Christ, who is the great antetype of Eliakim, has the key to the door of service and opportunity and to all the treasures of heaven, and He has the only power to open or close, according to His sovereign will.

Philadelphia was the youngest of the seven cities to which John was told to write. Philadelphia means "brotherly love." The city was founded three centuries earlier, because of its strategic location, to spread Greek culture and language to the provinces of Lydia and Phrygia. Likewise, these Philadelphian Christians had an open door of missionary opportunity to spread the message of Jesus Christ.

Located on a fertile volcanic plain where earthquakes and aftershocks were frequent, Philadelphia became known as the "city full of earthquakes." Most Philadelphians had chosen to live outside the city walls after it was completely destroyed again in A.D. 17. The fertile volcanic soil produced outstanding grapes and fine wine.

Philadelphia was a free Greek city with a few Christians living in the midst of a pagan people. It was the center of worship of the god Dionysus (later called Bacchus) and had temples to many other gods as well. Persecution of these Christians was severe, coming partly from the Romans, but mostly from the Jews. In spite of the paganism and persecution in the first century, because of the faithfulness of these early Christians, there is still a Christian presence there.

The angel of this church referred to Christ as holy, the description of God himself (Isaiah 6:3; 43:15; Revelation 6:10). Jesus was holy at birth (Luke 1:35), holy in death (Acts 2:27), and holy today, the eternal High Priest interceding on our behalf before God (Hebrews 7:26). And He is true (John 6:32-33). *The Reader's Digest Great Encyclopedic Dictionary* records many attributes of a person who is true: genuine, not counterfeit; faithful to friends, promises, principles, and the requirements of law or justice; loyal; steadfast.[1] William Barclay writes, "When we are confronted with [Jesus], we are confronted with no shadowy outline of the truth but with the truth itself."[2] Jesus himself declared that He is the Truth (John 14:6).

No one could shut the open door Jesus had put before this church in Philadelphia because they *have a little power, and have kept [His] word, and have not denied [His] name. A little power* is not a rebuke, but rather a commendation. Apparently they were small in number and without wealth or prominence. Yet amid great paganism, opposition, and persecution, they had been faithful in their deeds, had kept Christ's Word, and had not denied His name. Jesus had given them an open door of opportunity to spread His gospel and no one could close this door as long as the church remained faithful—no human, no demonic force!

In the second half of the 20th century, the Republic of China tried vigorously to close the door to Christianity. Christian missionaries were banned, and churches and all worship of the true God forbidden. Chinese Christian leaders and other followers of Christ were persecuted, imprisoned, and even executed. Despite this severe opposition, many Chinese Christians remained faithful, meeting secretly in homes, quietly sharing their faith. The doors to the church buildings may be shut and padlocked, but the true church in China is still alive. The enemy of Jesus Christ cannot shut the door; Jesus alone has the key.

4. Look up "faithful" in a dictionary, and record the definition.

Dear Lord, find me faithful.

> *Oh, may all who come behind us find us faithful.*
> *May the fire of our devotion light their way.*
> *May the footprints that we leave lead them to believe,*
> *And the lives we live inspire them to obey.*
> *Oh, may all who come behind us find us faithful.**
>
> —Jon Mohr

What does the Lord pardon?

Forever Promise

Read Revelation 3:7-13, concentrating on verses 9-13.

1. Look up "forever" in your dictionary, and write a brief definition.

2. Christ condemns those who say they are Jews and are not, who lie about it. What will He make them do?

3. Who is the true Jew and true descendant of Abraham in God's eyes? Use Romans 2:28-29 and Romans 9:6-8 to help you with your answer.

4. From what does Christ promise to keep His faithful followers (Revelation 3:10)?

5. Why does He urge them in verse 11 to *hold fast what you have?*

6. What will be the rewards for the overcomer?

False religion is always a formidable foe of true Christian faith. It had been Jewish religious leaders who had opposed Jesus and demanded His execution. Paul and other Early Church leaders had experienced opposition from the Jews. There were many Jews living in Philadelphia, and they were actively opposing and persecuting the Christians. Christ refers to them as *the synagogue of Satan* (verse 9) and promises that someday they will be humbled and will bow down before Him and His followers.

To God, the true Jew is the one who accepts and follows Jesus Christ, and the true descendant of Abraham is the person who has the faith of Abraham. All the promises made to Israel have now been inherited by the Church!

Jesus gave this faithful church in Philadelphia some wonderful promises, promises for each one of us who keeps

His Word and patiently endures, who perseveres and overcomes despite opposition and persecution. He promised to keep them from the hour of trial and testing that would come upon the whole world and everyone in it. Many believe this means that He will keep the faithful from going through this time of severe testing by removing them before it begins. Others believe it means that He will watch over and keep the faithful through that time. Whatever our belief, the important thing we need to remember is that He has promised to keep us. When we face trials and persecution, we can place our faith and trust in Jesus and His keeping power (2 Thessalonians 3:3).

When the disciples asked Jesus what would be the sign of His coming and the end of the age (Matthew 24:3), He tells them of trials and tribulations to come and that *most people's love will grow cold. But the one who endures to the end, he will be saved* (Matthew 24:12-13).

7. What will give us the strength to endure *to the end?* Summarize Hebrews 12:1-3.

When trials come, our nation becomes more and more secular, and Christianity is ridiculed and cast aside, we must be very careful not to condone or follow worldly attitudes. We must stay vigilant to guard against allowing even legitimate desires to become more important to us than following and obeying Christ. If we keep our eyes on Him and remain faithful, He provides us with (1) an example, (2) inspiration, and (3) comfort and strength for the times we must endure oppression (Hebrews 2:18).

He will come quickly! This does not mean "soon," but suddenly, unexpectedly, *like a thief in the night* (1 Thessalonians 5:2). We don't know the time of His second coming; we must always be ready. God measures time in terms of eternity, and a period of 2,000 years or more could still be "soon" or "quickly." (See 2 Peter 3:8-9.) We must keep our eyes fixed on Jesus and persevere faithfully and obediently to the end, that we might not lose "the crown of righteousness." (See 2 Timothy 4:7-8 and Revelation 3:11.)

Jesus will make the overcomer a permanent pillar in God's temple. A pillar represents strength, stability, and permanence. (In many of the remains of the ancient cities in this part of the world, only the pillars of their buildings still remain.) This had special meaning to these Christians in earthquake-prone Philadelphia, who frequently had to flee the city because of tremors. We often refer to a person of spiritual strength, stability, and reliability as "a pillar of the church." (See Galatians 2:9.) God the Father and Jesus, His Son, the Lamb of God, will be the only temple in the New Jerusalem (Revelation 21:22), and the one who overcomes will have oneness with them and permanently be in their presence (3:12).

Jesus will write these names on the overcomer:

1. *The name of God.* God's name had first been placed on the Israelites (Numbers 6:24-27) and signified ownership. We will wear His name, the badge that indicates that we belong to God.

2. *The name of the city of God.* We will wear the name of the New Jerusalem, where we will have permanent citizenship, security, love, joy, peace, community, and the presence of God for eternity (Ezekiel 48:35).

3. *The new name of Jesus, "which no one knows except Himself" (Revelation 19:12).* We will have fuller knowledge of and communication with Christ. Jesus is His redemptive name, and His redemptive work will no longer be required. He will have a new work to do and a new name.

Are you ready for the return of our Lord Jesus Christ to catch His bride (the Church) away? Are you His faithful and obedient servant? If not, take a few moments right now to ask God to forgive your sins and empower you to persevere and endure faithfully in radical obedience to His will.

Thank You, Lord, for Your keeping power and loving guidance. Give me strength to endure faithfully any trials Satan places in my path.

MEMORY CHALLENGE

Fill in the blanks:

Bless _____ _____, O my _____, and all

_____ is _____ ____, bless _____ _____

_____. Bless _____ _____, O _____ _____,

and forget _____ of His _____; who _____ all

your _____, who _____ all your _____.
                                                    Psalm 103:1-3

DAY FIVE

Fashionable Church

Read Revelation 3:14-22, concentrating on verses 14-18.

1. To which church is Jesus sending this message?

2. What words and phrases does Jesus use to identify himself?

3. Jesus described the condition of the church at Laodicea as neither _____ nor _____, but _____.

4. The members of this church saw themselves as rich and in need of nothing. How did Jesus see them?

5. Do you believe this same self-deception has relevance for the Church today? Why?

6. Read Matthew 5:13-14, 16. Jesus said, *You are the salt of the earth. . . . You are the light of the world* (verses 13-14). What happens to salt that has become tasteless?

What should we do with the light we have been given?

7. Name the three things Jesus told the church in Laodicea to "buy" from Him, and tell what each would do for them.

8. What is your personal spiritual temperature? Cold, lukewarm, or hot—on fire and eager to serve Jesus and to win the lost? Are you salt and light in a lost and dying world? If you don't know Christ as your Lord and Savior (cold), ask Him to forgive your sins—accept His loving grace, and become His child. If you've lost the eagerness and fervency in your relationship with Christ (lukewarm), ask Him to forgive you and to *restore . . .*

the joy of [His] salvation (Psalm 51:12). Prayerfully read Psalms 51:1-17 and 139:23-24.

I know you inside and out, and find little to my liking. You're not cold, you're not hot—far better to be either cold or hot! You're stale. You're stagnant. You make me want to vomit. You brag, "I'm rich, I've got it made, I need nothing from anyone," oblivious that in fact you're a pitiful, blind beggar, threadbare and homeless (Revelation 3:15-17, TM).

Laodicea was one of the wealthiest cities in the world, known for its commerce, its Greek culture, science, literature, and medicine. It was famous for the unusually beautiful woolen clothing and carpets made from a soft, glossy, violet-black wool that came from locally raised sheep. It was the financial and banking center of Asia. It was also a great trading center, located literally astride the road from Ephesus to Syria, the most important road in Asia. Two other roads passed through the city for a total of three major trade routes.

The church at Laodicea is the only one of the seven churches about which Christ has no word of commendation. The church had adopted the philosophy of the city. "Laodicea" means "the will or rule of the people," and a popular phrase was *vox populi, vox Dei*, which translates to "The voice of the people is the voice of God."

There is no evidence that Paul ever visited Laodicea, but the church was in his thoughts and prayers (Colossians 2:1; 4:13, 15), and when he wrote to the Colossian church from the Roman prison, he asked that his letter be read to the Laodiceans (Colossians 4:16).

There was a large Jewish population in Laodicea, but the spiritual battles of this church were neither with *the synagogue of Satan* nor with the Roman government nor with false teachers; their battle was within their own hearts.

In this message to the church at Laodicea, Jesus refers to himself as "the Amen." Jesus used this expression often to affirm the truth of what He was preparing to say to His followers. It was usually translated "verily" or "truly." As an ending to prayer, it means "So be it." It is a guarantee of truth; the promises of Jesus are true and will be fulfilled. When Jesus speaks, it is the final word; He is the truth (John 1:14; 14:6). Christ is *the faithful and true Witness* (Revelation 3:14); we can rely on His Word. He does not dilute (He's faithful) nor distort (He's true) the Word of God. In contrast, the church at Laodicea was neither faithful nor true.

Christ was Creator of all the material things that were so important to these Laodiceans (John 1:1-3; Colossians 1:16). He is able to see through our disguises and see us as we really are, the sham and shallowness of our lives, the pretenses and self-indulgence. He knows when we love the created things of the world more than the Creator and worship them.

The word translated "lukewarm" refers to tepid water, and this is the only time it is used in the New Testament. There was no source of water inside the city of Laodicea; it received its water from ice-cold springs in nearby mountains by way of an aqueduct. When it reached the city it was lukewarm. Water from boiling springs near the city was also tepid when it reached Laodicea and could cause those who drank it to become ill.

A lukewarm attitude is usually one of compromise and an absence of genuine spiritual fervor. Lukewarm people are those who have been touched by the gospel and may be professing Christians who attend church regularly, but the fire has gone out. They are merely pew-sitters with no active involvement, those who want to be comfortable rather than challenged. They are not cold toward Christ but aren't the radically obedient and enthusiastic disciples Jesus calls His followers to be. They have drifted into a conventional and meaningless Christianity, willing to compromise with worldly attitudes in order to stay in a religious comfort zone. This is lukewarm "churchianity," not true Christianity, and it makes Jesus want to spit it out of His mouth (vomit).

What does Jesus tell us we must do to keep the fire of our salvation burning? We must walk closely and prayerfully with Him, read and meditate on God's Word—abide in Jesus. Prayerfully read John 15:1-11.

Indifference is an attitude Christ condemns. It is harder to combat than outright antagonism against Him. Christianity and the Church often have little relevance to the world, because the world fails to see a demonstration of the power of Christianity or of the grace it provides to make life abundant and beautiful. Jesus said that we are to be salt and light to a hurting, lost world. If our "flavor" has diminished and our "light" is dimmed, we are of little use to Jesus. We may be ridiculed, challenged, and confronted, or even persecuted for our commitment, but we dare not be complacent and compromised.

Lord, help me to be committed, not complacent, in my relationship with You.

MEMORY CHALLENGE

What does the Lord heal?

DAY SIX

Fervent Plea

Read Revelation 3:19-22.

1. Who does Jesus reprove and discipline?

2. Record these verses:

   Job 5:17

   Proverbs 3:12

   Proverbs 13:24

   Hebrews 12:10

3. God loves you. When you are convinced of His love, you are able to accept His reproof and discipline in the right spirit. Prayerfully read John 3:16-17 with 1 John 4:7-21, and record a verse that is especially meaningful to you. If you are comfortable doing so, share with your group.

4. With what honor will Jesus reward the overcomer (Revelation 3:21)?

Christ condemns this church at Laodicea for being lukewarm and self-satisfied, but He still loves these people, and His reproof is not for punishment but for illumination. He rebukes them because He loves them and wants them to see themselves as He sees them and to change their ways. After God rebuked David for his sin with Bathsheba, speaking through the words of the prophet Nathan, David accepted the reproof, acknowledged his sin before God, and sought forgiveness: *Wash me thoroughly from my iniquity and cleanse me from my sin. For I know my transgressions, and my sin is ever before me* (Psalm 51:2-3).

"Discipline" is a word that means "to train and instruct in order to bring about a change of attitude and character." William Barclay in *The Daily Study Bible Series* wrote, "The discipline of God is not something we should resent, but something for which we should be devoutly thankful."[1]

"Repentance" means "turning to God"; its meaning, however, also includes turning away from what is displeasing to God, and genuine sorrow over the sinful act or attitude.
The people I love, I call to account—prod and correct and guide so that they'll live at their best. Up on your feet, then! About face! Run after God!

Look at me. I stand at the door. I knock. If you hear me call and open the door, I'll come right in and sit down to supper with you. Conquerors will sit alongside me at the head table, just as I, having conquered, took the place of honor at the side of my Father. That's my gift to the conquerors! (Revelation 3:20-21, TM).

The Light of the World is a famous painting by Holman Hunt. Jesus is depicted standing outside a door, holding a lighted lantern in one hand and, with His other hand extended, knocking on the door. A story has been told of one of the artist's friends who admired the newly completed painting but pointed out what he thought was a mistake: There was no handle or knob on the door, no way it could be opened. Hunt replied that it was not a mistake—the door to one's heart can be opened only from the inside.

The Lord is pleading for admittance. No other religion worships a God who is a seeker of men or who grieves over those who reject Him. He is available right now to restore fellowship with the church or the individual who earnestly repents for the self-sufficiency and apathy that denies the need for a vital relationship with God. Jesus knocks at the door of each and every heart. Have you opened the door of *your* heart and invited Him in? If not, He's patiently and lovingly knocking. Invite Him in. Fellowship with Jesus is the greatest joy you'll ever know.

If we confess our sins, He is faithful and righteous to forgive us our sins and to cleanse us from all unrighteousness (1 John 1:9).

These messages to the seven churches are also meant for us—the stern rebukes and the loving promises. The Holy Spirit is speaking to us through these words, and the message is as relevant and challenging now as it was 1,900 years ago. *He who has an ear, let him hear what the Spirit says to the churches* (Revelation 2:7, 11, 17, 29, and 3:6, 13, 22).

Written by Helen Silvey

MEMORY CHALLENGE

Recite Psalm 103:1-3 aloud.

Revelation

LESSON 4

■ A Study of Revelation 4

Doors

Read Revelation 4:1-11, concentrating on verse 1.

1. In verse 1, what did John see?

2. There are a number of applications for the word "door" in the Bible. Record phrases showing how "door" is used in these verses:

   Psalm 141:3

   Hosea 2:15

   Luke 13:24

   John 10:7

   Acts 14:27

   1 Corinthians 16:9

   Colossians 4:3

   Revelation 3:8

   Revelation 3:20

In the New Testament Jesus calls himself *the door* (John 10:7, 9). Faith in Him is the only way to enter the kingdom of God. God gave to the Gentiles *a door of faith,* or an opportunity to know Him as Lord (Acts 14:27). Paul constantly sought *a wide door for effective service,* an occasion for ministry in the name of Christ (1 Corinthians 16:9). Jesus stands at the door and knocks (Revelation 3:20). He calls all of us to himself but will not enter the door of our hearts without our permission. We must open the door for Him before He can open the door of heaven for us.

3. God will one day open the door for us as He did for John in his vision; the trumpet will sound, and God's people will be called to heaven. Record 1 Thessalonians 4:17.

4. Meanwhile, we must take advantage of the open door of faithful service He gives us. Personalize the following verses by inserting your name in the appropriate places.

   Matthew 5:16

   Colossians 1:10

   1 Peter 2:12

Psalm 103:4

*Who redeems your life
from the pit,
who crowns you with
lovingkindness and compassion.*

Are you entering doors that you should close? Is there a closed door that you should enter?

In our study of Revelation, God is revealing a closed door that must be opened. He has used Paul Marshall's book *Their Blood Cries Out* to say, *He who has ears to hear, let him hear.*

> It is Sunday morning in Sudan, in China, in Nepal, in Iran, in Cuba. . . .
>
> Some . . . make their way across their villages to attend worship services. . . . Intent as they are on gathering together with other believers, they know full well that they may pay dearly for doing so.
>
> Others arise with the dawn, assemble their poorly-fed children inside shabby homes, and those that have them read quickly from well-worn Bibles that remain carefully hidden during the week. They pray for their daily bread and for the courage to carry on.
>
> Still others encounter the first day of the week in the darkness of their prison cells. Prayer is on their lips, too, as they look forward to further interrogation, torture and perhaps eventually execution.
>
> Meanwhile, in America, a somewhat different scene unfolds. . . . Worshipers in air-conditioned buildings, . . . in upholstered pews, eagerly receive the Good News. Encouraging words are offered in myriad sermons, dramatic presentation and testimonials. The message is televised, recorded in countless books and on audio tapes. It is sung in anthems, cried out in rock tunes and chanted in gospel choruses. It is expressed with tearful promises, with witty anecdotes or with pop-psych platitudes. The promise is one of peace.
>
> The beatings, looting, torture, jailing, enslavement, murder and even crucifixion of increasingly vulnerable Christian communities is met with silence and indifference of the Western world.[1]

Rev. David Stravers, vice president of the Bible League, gives two reasons for American Christians' relative lack of interest in the plight of suffering sisters and brothers worldwide:

1. American Christians, for the most part, are not interested in anything that happens outside the boundaries of the United States, and in many cases, outside the boundaries of their own communities.

2. American Christians have no experience of persecution or suffering for their faith that even remotely resembles the experiences of many of our overseas brothers and sisters. It is difficult to empathize when many, many, many American Christians refuse to believe what's reported because it's so far outside their experience.[2]

Scriptures give us clear guidelines for addressing persecution. First and foremost, we are called to concerted prayer. When Peter and Paul were in prison, the entire church gathered to pray for their release. Beyond the call to prayer is the call to action. Jesus left the 99 sheep to go look for the lost one. Action is also taken in the parable of the Good Samaritan. In striking contrast to the priest, who took the easy road of prayer alone, the Samaritan stopped his equally busy journey to extend the love of Christ to the wounded. Galatians 6:10 tells us, *As we have opportunity, let us do good to all people, especially to those who belong to the family of believers* (NIV).

What does God require of us when our Christian brothers and sisters are suffering and dying? How would we react if a loved one was sacrificing his or her life to answer God's call to preach the gospel under these circumstances?

We could pray and recruit others to join us. We could contact authorities in our government to inform them and request aid from them. We could find organizations fighting religious persecution and work with them to do anything we could to remedy human suffering.

Shouldn't we begin now to respond to these tragedies? This is a door that we should open and never close.

For further information, contact these United States offices of groups fighting religious persecution:

Open Doors with Brother Andrew
P.O. Box 27000
Santa Ana, CA 92799
(714-531-6000)
(a large international, evangelical organization formed to help suffering Christians throughout the world)

Compass Direct News Service
P.O. Box 27250
Santa Ana, CA 92799
(a highly informative newsletter on the persecution of Christians, published by Open Doors)

The Voice of the Martyrs
P.O. Box 443
Bartlesville, OK 74005
(918-337-8015)
(a large international Christian association serving the persecuted Church in over 50 countries)

Heaven

Read Revelation 4:1.

1. Where was the open door?

2. Who dwells in heaven?

   Isaiah 66:1

   Matthew 23:9

   Matthew 28:2

   Mark 16:19

3. Who can enter heaven?

   Matthew 5:3

   Matthew 25:31-40

   1 Peter 1:3-5

4. Who cannot enter heaven?

   John 3:3

   John 3:16-18

   1 Corinthians 6:9-10

5. Record Revelation 4:1.

Can you imagine the indescribable joy of hearing *the . . . voice . . . like the sound of a trumpet speaking [to us, saying], "Come up here"*?

In chapter 1 of Revelation John was instructed to write. He wrote to the seven churches on earth. Now in chapter 4 he is being told to *come up here*. John is leaving the earth and entering into heaven and will see some of the glories that are waiting for all Christians. A friend explained to me her condensed version of Revelation—she said that we can read Revelation from the beginning to the end, and we'll learn that its basic message is "Get ready." Are *you* ready?

In his newspaper column Billy Graham gave wise counsel to a soon-to-be college graduate's question about his future:

The most important thing I can say to you is to urge you to seek God's will for your life. He created you and knows all about you and your future; doesn't it make sense, therefore, to let Him guide you?

What is God's will? God's will, first of all, is for you to put your life into His hands by turning to Christ and asking Him to be the foundation and center of all you do. As Jesus said, "My Father's will is that everyone who looks to the Son and believes in him shall have eternal life" (John 6:40 [NIV]).

God's will is for you to seek His plan for your life and then do it. God knows your abilities (and also your limitations), and He knows what is right for you. Trust Him to guide you. The Bible says, "Trust in the LORD with all your heart and lean not on your own understanding; in all your ways acknowledge him, and he will make your paths straight" (Proverbs 3:5-6 [NIV]).

There is no greater joy in life than being in the will of God. Sometimes it is hard to discern His will, but when we sincerely seek Him and truly want His will, He can be trusted to direct us and help us.[1]

As I read Dr. Graham's answer, I remembered that eternal life began for me when I made a total commitment of my life to the Lord. Of course, my Christian walk is not perfect, but the Holy Spirit continually reassures me with His presence, and He makes it a heavenly walk on earth. I know that I am ready to hear *the . . . voice . . . like the sound of a trumpet speaking [to us, saying], "Come up here"* (Revelation 4:1).

Are you ready? If you have even the slightest doubt, turn to 1 John 1:8-9 and obey His words.

Dear God, remind us of unconfessed sin so that we can ask forgiveness from You and be ready when we hear "Come up here." In Jesus' name we pray. Amen.

Fill in the blanks:

Who redeems your life from the _____, who crowns you with lovingkindness and _____.

Psalm 103:4

DAY THREE

His Voice

Read Revelation 4:1.

1. How does John describe the voice he is hearing?

2. How are prophetic Scriptures given to believers (2 Peter 1:20-21)?

3. Jesus' most repeated statement (15 times in the New Testament) was *He who has ears to hear, let him hear.* What do the following verses tell us about hearing the Lord?

   Luke 8:21

   John 8:47

   John 10:27

   Revelation 3:20

4. One of the strongest teachings of the New Testament is that God the Holy Spirit lives in the believer now, to be to the believer all that Jesus was to the disciples. What do the following Scriptures tell us about the Holy Spirit?

   John 14:16

   John 14:17

   John 16:8

   1 John 2:27

The person who is listening to the Holy Spirit and acting on what he or she hears is the person who will hear more and more from the Lord. This is not because God speaks to such persons more often but because they have developed the ability to hear God more clearly. They act positively on the smallest impression from the Lord. To ignore or refuse to act on guidance from the Holy Spirit weakens our sensitivity to His voice.

Christians are called to see Him who is invisible and hear Him who is voiceless. Every day we should determine to remember that the Holy Spirit of God is always with us. He rides beside us as we drive to work. He watches us as we sleep. He is the One who selects the circumstances of our life. At any moment, He is ready to impart courage, peace, forgiveness, protection, wisdom, and help in time of need.

A few months ago, I felt drawn to accept a responsibility that I had never considered being able to do. At first I ignored the urging because it seemed so impossible. When the urging continued, I began to search the Scriptures for guidance. Because of my feelings of inadequacy, I hoped He would show me I was wrong. The words that spoke clearly to me were found in Psalm 32:8-9, which says, *I will instruct you and teach you in the way which you should go; I will counsel you with My eye upon you. Do not be as the horse or as the mule which have no understanding, whose trappings include bit and bridle to hold them in check.* I decided that if I refused, God would consider me as stubborn as a mule! It was still a few weeks before I could say, "I'll try." Today it is the most exciting and fulfilling responsibility I have.

Thank You, dear Lord, for Your patience and mercy in showing us, through Your Holy Spirit, Your will for us now.

Recently I needed to cross a busy expressway. I stopped, looked both ways, and, seeing no cars, began to cross the street. Suddenly I felt very strongly impressed to stop, so I did. I watched in amazement as a small car seemingly came from nowhere and sped by me on the expressway.

His love for us goes beyond all our understanding. His care for us can never be fully known. Our failure to develop a closer and deeper relationship with Him disappoints and saddens Him. We rob ourselves of a joy-filled life when we let the world and our own self-centeredness crowd Him out of first place in our lives and we can no longer hear His voice.

MEMORY CHALLENGE

When my life is in the pit, what can God do for me? What crown will He let me wear?

DAY FOUR

In the Spirit

Read Revelation 4:2.

1. Record Revelation 4:2.

"*In the Spirit* means John was worshiping. It does not mean he was in a state of high ecstasy. He was honoring God, thinking about Him, and paying tribute to His majesty, His greatness, and His power."[1]

Worship is characterized by a freedom within one's spirit to receive a greater awareness of His holiness and a willingness to receive new creativity in ministry and solutions to life's situations. There is a yieldedness and longing to be shown any sin or area to be corrected.

2. There are certain action steps we must take before we can enter into worship. Record the five action steps listed in James 4:7-8.

   (1)

   (2)

   (3)

   (4)

   (5)

To submit to God, we must submit to the whole counsel of God. We cannot follow God and the world at the same time. Summarize Matthew 6:24.

We must resist the devil because a Christian's enemies are the demonic spirits of Satan. Summarize the following:

   Ephesians 6:11-12

   1 Peter 5:8-9

To draw near to God is to grow closer to Him continually. Summarize the following:

   Jeremiah 29:12-14

   Hebrews 10:22

To *cleanse your hands* (James 4:8) is to repent of your sins. Summarize the following:

   Psalm 24:3-4

   1 John 1:7

To purify our hearts means that with a clean heart we become single-minded for the Lord. Summarize James 1:7-8.

To try to follow God and the world at the same time is double-minded behavior. We need a pure, undivided heart if we want to worship and hear God. With a pure heart, our perception of God is clear and definite, and our communication with Him will be more sure. A hearing ear and a pure heart are basic necessities for us to hear the Father speak.

3. Record Matthew 5:8.

To worship God in the Spirit is a process that requires discipline. Satan can be counted on to make us uncomfortable and will cause every distraction he can to get our minds off of worshiping and hearing God.

The goal of our worship should be that we come to the place at which we're not aware of anyone or anything around us but become totally focused on God. John was truly worshiping when he received the vision from God.

Our walk in obedience to God's Word takes us from a life of self-centeredness to a life of Christ-centeredness. A self-centered person can never experience true worship. We must develop a life of worship, living in His presence constantly, not just in corporate worship on Sunday. John 4:23-24 tells us the Father seeks those who worship Him in Spirit and truth. He longs for our worship. He wants communion with us.

Characteristics of authentic worship:

1. *Worship God alone.* Record Exodus 20:3.

2. *Love God with all your heart.* Record Deuteronomy 6:5.

3. *Depend on the Holy Spirit.* Summarize John 16:13.

4. *Focus on praise.* Record Psalm 34:1.

Read Luke 19:37-40 from *The Living Bible.* Record verse 40.

5. Balance seriousness with joyful enthusiasm. Summarize 1 Chronicles 16:25.

6. Avoid all sin. Summarize 1 Corinthians 10:13.

7. Concentrate on unity and order. Record 1 Corinthians 14:40.

We can study and learn from David's experience of worship in 2 Samuel 6:1-20. David had a strong desire to be in God's presence. Knowing His presence was enthroned above the cherubim of the ark of God, David gathered 30,000 chosen men of Israel to go with him to Baale-judah to bring the ark of God home to Jerusalem. As they traveled toward Jerusalem with the ark, he and other leaders of Israel were joyously waving branches of juniper trees and playing every kind of musical instrument before the Lord—lyres, harps, tambourines, castanets, and cymbals. Their worship involved their whole being (2 Samuel 6:5).

As they continued their journey to Jerusalem, David bal-

anced their enthusiastic celebrating with times of sacrificial offerings and his blessing of the people in the name of the Lord of hosts. Read 2 Samuel 6:16, 20-23 to learn of the reaction of Michal, David's wife, to David's celebration of worship of God.
1. Michal failed to enter into worship.
2. Michal scorned David and those worshiping.
3. Michal had a prideful heart.

Michal would not worship with David and the leaders of Israel because they were not worshiping in the way she was taught in the house of Saul, her father. Not only did she not worship, but she scorned those who were worshiping. Her prideful heart would not allow worship except in the way she thought it ought to be done.

The attitude of Michal is prevalent today and is one we must guard against. We're not all alike or in the same place in our relationship to God. We must give freedom to those who worship God in ways different from us. We're loving and worshiping the same God, the Heavenly Father of us all.

How can you begin today to make praise and worship of God a more regular part of your life?

Father, I want to worship You in spirit and truth. Help me! In Jesus' name I pray. Amen.

MEMORY CHALLENGE

Fill in the blanks:

Bless the _____, O my soul, and all that is _____ _____, bless _____ _____ _____. Bless the _____, O my soul, and _____ none of _____ _____; who _____ all your _____, who _____ all your _____; who _____ your life _____ the _____; who _____ you with _____ and _____.

Psalm 103:1-4

The Throne of God

Read Revelation 4:2-5.

1. In verse 2, what did John see?

2. Describe the Occupant of the throne (verse 3).

3. What do the brilliance and the color of *a jasper stone and a sardius* suggest about the One on the throne? (Refer to Psalm 104:1.)

4. What is seen around the throne, and how is it described?

5. John sees 24 elders seated upon 24 thrones that surround the throne of God. What do their white garments signify?

6. What is indicated by their golden crowns? (Hint: see 2 Timothy 4:8.)

7. What suggests terrible judgment will go forth from the throne (verse 5)?

John's vision is filled with Old Testament symbols and experiences. We find similarities to the vision of Isaiah in the year King Uzziah died (Isaiah 6:1-5), and there are even more similarities to the vision of Ezekiel (Ezekiel 1).

The green jasper (jade) and red sardius (carnelian) are reminders of the breastplate stones of the high priest, described in Exodus 28:17-21.

The rainbow—*a halo like an emerald rainbow* (verse 3, PHILLIPS) reminds us of both Noah's rainbow (Genesis 9:16-17) and Ezekiel's mention of a rainbow (Ezekiel 1:28). The 24 elders may refer to the 24 priestly divisions who conducted the worship of Israel according to the traditions of the Levites. They seem to represent the saints of God in their act of worship, just as the Levitical priests represented Israel in the worship at the Temple.

Flashes of lightning and sounds and peals of thunder (verse 5) are the sights and sounds associated with the giving of the Law on Mount Sinai (Exodus 19:16). These sounds are a symbol of God's judgments.

What is there in these Scriptures that has value for us in this day?

In his study of Revelation, Ray C. Stedman believed that what John saw is what we will see when we're taken up to be with Christ.

> Heaven is not some distant planet. Heaven is another dimension of existence right here and now. When John saw a door opened into heaven, he was permitted to see into a realm that is present all the time and governs the visible affairs of earth.
>
> The first thing John saw was a throne. It's very important to remember that all the events that take place on earth somehow relate to that central throne where God rules in His universe. We must never forget that behind all human events is the government of God.
>
> The fact that there's a throne means there are absolutes that cannot be altered or changed. They are guaranteed by the authority of the throne. Nothing anyone does can alter them in the least degree. There are scientific absolutes that scientists must work around. There are moral absolutes that cannot be altered, no matter how far society may drift. God maintains these absolutes constantly from His throne. Amid the great tumult of his days, Jeremiah declared, *A glorious throne on high from the beginning is the place of our sanctuary* (Jeremiah 17:12). That is the throne John saw.[1]

Our God reigns! That is the theme of Revelation.

Write out Psalm 103:1-4 from memory.

The Worship of God

Read Revelation 4:6-11.

1. What kind of creatures were *in the center and around the throne?*

2. How were the four living creatures around the throne similar?

3. What attribute of God did the four living creatures praise again and again?

4. How did the 24 elders worship the Lord God?

5. What attitudes do you think are expressed by falling down before God?

6. Why did the elders say that God was worthy of their worship?

7. Based on this chapter, what seems to be an important occupation in heaven?

In the center and around the throne are four living creatures who work at leading creation to worship its Creator. The creatures are like winged animals, covered with eyes all over their bodies, even under their wings. Ezekiel saw similar creatures, which he calls cherubim. Cherubim are not little plump, naked babies with miniwings that fly around and shoot people with love arrows. They are like the creatures that John describes. Isaiah calls them seraphim. They appear in different configurations—some with six wings, others with four. The eyes on the creatures tell us they are all-seeing and all-wise; the wings show they are ready for service and are quick to respond.

Many symbolic meanings have been seen in the four living creatures. We will look at four of them.

1. The four living creatures may be superior beings intended to represent all living creatures: the lion representing wild beasts; the ox, domestic animals; the face of a man, humanity; and the eagle, birds of the air.

2. The four may be representative of Christ: the lion representing His authority; the ox, His sacrifice (since the ox is a sacrificial animal); the man, His humanity; and the eagle, His divinity.

3. Some see in the four living creatures the four Gospels: Matthew is best represented by the lion, because in the Gospel of Matthew, Jesus is depicted as the Lion of Judah. Mark is best represented by the man, because his Gospel is the nearest to the physical facts of the life of Je-

sus. Luke is best represented by the ox, because he depicts Jesus as the sacrifice for all classes and conditions of men and women everywhere. John is best represented by the eagle, because, of all the birds, the eagle flies highest and is said to be the only living creature that can look straight into the sun; and John of all the Gospels reaches the highest heights of thought.

4. A fourth possibility is that the creatures are representative of the attributes of God: the lion representing His power; the ox, His sacrificial love; the man, His incarnation; and the eagle, His sovereignty.

This is one of the places in the Book of Revelation where we cannot be sure of the proper interpretation. But whatever the creatures represent, they never cease praising God. Their presence in heaven gives a greater awareness of the majesty, holiness, sovereignty, and eternity of God.

The closing scene of chapter 4 brings out several important truths. It is evident that the living creatures are designed to give glory, honor, and thanks to God. The emphasis of their praise is on the divine attributes and worthiness of God.

The worship given by the 24 elders recognizes these attributes of God as well as the fact that God is the sovereign Creator of the universe. Also, in casting their crowns before the throne, they are saying that if it had not been for God's grace, salvation, and goodness, they could not have had victory over sin and death. Here the creature is honoring His Maker and accepts the truth that humanity must be subject to its Creator.

Many people in the world today do not give such honor to the Lord God. Though they benefit from His goodness and live in a universe of His creation, they tend to neglect the worship of God. Wise is the soul who finds in the Scriptures the revelation of such a God and will bow now in this day of grace and begin to worship the God he or she will serve in eternity.

Written by Marie Coody

Quote Psalm 103:1-4 to someone in your discussion group.

Revelation

LESSON 5

■ **A Study of Revelation 5**

DAY ONE

Sinners

Read Revelation 5, concentrating on verses 1-3.

1. Where does Revelation 5 take place?

2. Describe what was in the right hand of Him who sat on the throne.

3. Point out the similarities of Revelation 5:1 and the following scriptures.

    Isaiah 29:11

    Ezekiel 2:9-10

    Daniel 12:4

4. What was the question the angel asked?

5. Are any of us worthy of what God has to offer us? Summarize the following scriptures to help with your answer.

    Matthew 8:7-8

    Luke 15:21

    John 1:26-27

6. Who was worthy to open the book (verse 3)?

7. Record the following scriptures.

    Psalm 51:3

    Luke 5:8

    Romans 3:23

Revelation 5 is a chapter of high drama. The scene is in heaven, where God himself holds a scroll in His right hand. The scroll is symbolic of a title to the earth. The fact that it is written on both sides shows its importance and the comprehensive nature of its contents. The scroll is obviously valuable, for it is sealed with seven seals that must each be broken separately and in order. Whoever can take the scroll receives the right to rule the earth.

You will notice in verse 2 that the angel asked, *Who is worthy?* not "Who is willing?" Alexander the Great, Napoleon, and Hitler were all willing to rule the earth, but they were not worthy. Righteous men such as the apostle Paul, Martin Luther, or Billy Graham could not even be considered worthy. In the next verse we learn that *no one in heaven or on the earth or under the earth was able to open the book or to look into it.* Not one of us, no matter how hard we try or how righteous we become, are worthy. To God, our own righteousness is like filthy rags.

MEMORY CHALLENGE

Psalm 103:5

Who satisfies your years with good things, so that your youth is renewed like the eagle.

It is interesting to note that Revelation 5 summarizes the entire story of the Bible in one chapter. First, we see God sitting on the throne as the One who has created everything, including earth, all that is in it, and humanity. We realize that humanity was created to have fellowship with Him but that fellowship was broken through sin. God wanted to restore His relationship with humanity and needed someone who was worthy to restore it by taking title to the earth and humanity. But throughout the ages, not one person has ever been worthy. Even the greatest of God's men and women failed Him at various times. Then the Lion of Judah appears, who becomes the Lamb for sinners slain. He earns the title of Savior. Because He restores humanity's relationship to God, He gives us a new song to sing, a song of joy and praise. We have an opportunity to give honor and glory to God. The entire chapter reflects the sovereignty of God. He and He alone is worthy and reigns and has everything under His control.

Revelation 5 shows the progression of God's plan. Yet, it is written in the future and then replays the past. It required that the Savior be slain, for God required blood sacrifice to cover sins, but the Savior was willing. This is the story of Christ's death on the Cross for our redemption. We praise and worship the Father, Son, and Holy Spirit. Truly, He is the sovereign God who holds heaven and earth in His hand, just as He holds the book in verse 1. He controls the past, present, and future and does so with lovingkindness, faithfulness, and trustworthiness.

We are saved not because we deserve it but because of God's incredible grace. As the slain Lamb, Jesus Christ covers us with His blood, which blots out our sin. We are worthy of punishment, but He who was without sin takes it on himself. This is grace for sinners. *It is a trustworthy statement, deserving full acceptance, that Christ Jesus came into the world to save sinners* (1 Timothy 1:15). *In Him we have redemption through His blood, the forgiveness of our trespasses, according to the riches of His grace which He lavished upon us* (Ephesians 1:7-8). *And the grace of our Lord was more than abundant, with the faith and love which are found in Christ Jesus* (1 Timothy 1:14). Therefore, *be strong in the grace that is in Christ Jesus* (2 Timothy 2:1).

DAY TWO

Savior

Read Revelation 5:4-5.

1. What was John's reaction when no one was found worthy?

2. Who did the elder say had *overcome?*

3. Look up the following scriptures, and list the points that help explain *the Lion that is from the tribe of Judah, the Root of David.* (Remember that Jesse was David's father.)

   Genesis 49:9

   Isaiah 11:10

   Revelation 22:16

4. Who is the Lion of Judah?

5. Summarize the following scriptures, which tell what the Lion of Judah did for us.

   Isaiah 53:5-6

   2 Corinthians 5:21

   1 John 2:12

6. Yesterday we were reminded that none of us are worthy of God's goodness to us. Today we see that in God's plan He sent a _____. Summarize the following scriptures.

   Philippians 3:20

   1 Timothy 4:10

Titus 2:13

7. What is the theme the above verses seem to have in
    common?

Peter was a little boy who lived in Holland, a low-lying
land that struggled against the sea. In order to have more
land, this small country put up high walls called dikes to
hold back the water. One night while riding his bike home
along the dike at dusk, Peter heard an unusual gurgling
noise. He looked down to see a leak in the dike near the
ground. Peter was alarmed, realizing that the hole would
only get bigger if left unattended. He tried putting a rock
or stick in the hole, but the pressure of the water immediately pushed it out. The only thing that seemed to work
was his thumb. So Peter kept his thumb in the dike while
he shouted for help.

Unfortunately, this was a seldom-traveled road, and few
were out at night. But Peter could not leave, so he fought
sleep and cold all night to keep his thumb in the dike.

Early in the morning, help finally came in the form of a
milkman on his wagon. Peter shouted for help, and the
milkman came, examined the hole, and ran to the village
for help. A crew of men came and repaired the dike, pro-
claiming Peter a hero. He was hailed as the savior of the
people because of his struggle to keep the sea from flood-
ing the land.

Mary Mapes Dodge made up this story over 130 years ago
for her children. It later became a part of her famous book
Hans Brinker or *The Silver Skates*. But while Mrs.
Dodge's story is fiction, God's story of a Savior is real. Sav-
iors like Peter are important but temporary, while God's
Savior is for all people and for all times. Christ's work on
earth was finished on the Cross, but Revelation promises
us the day will come when He will be crowned finally and
forever as Savior.

MEMORY CHALLENGE

Record Psalm 107:9, which relates to Psalm 103:5.

DAY THREE

Slain

Read Revelation 5:6-8.

1. Describe what John saw between the throne and the
    elders.

2. To understand the background of the Lamb, we need to
    study the Passover lamb. Explain the purpose of the
    Passover lamb as described in Exodus 12:1-13.

3. Scripture points to Christ as being the Lamb. Summa-
    rize each of the following.

    Isaiah 53:7

    John 1:28-29

    1 Peter 1:18-19

4. As you understand salvation, why did the Lamb have to
    be slain?

5. List some reasons the Lamb was worthy to be the one
    to take the book from the right hand of Him who sat on
    the throne. If possible, back up your reasons with scrip-
    ture.

6. What happened when the Lamb took the book?

Christ, the Lamb of God, chose to be slain for our sins. Sometimes this sounds so theological that we don't understand what it means. One morning during my devotions the Lord helped break it down for me this way:

In order to be slain or die on the Cross for our sins, Christ first had to humble himself. The *Guideposts Family Concordance* defines "humble" as "having a proper sense of one's worth."[1] Of all creatures, certainly Christ had the right to say, "There's no one more important than me! I'm God's Son!" But Jesus knew His worth was of no value without humility. Arrogance would have cost Him His purity and righteousness. Christ knew His sense of worth was in humility and in following His Father's plan. *Being found in appearance as a man, He humbled Himself by becoming obedient to the point of death, even death on a cross* (Philippians 2:8).

After Jesus humbled himself, He took on our sin, which He did not deserve. Romans 3:23 tells us that *all have sinned, and come short of the glory of God* (KJV)—all except God's Son, Jesus Christ. *For we do not have a high priest who cannot sympathize with our weaknesses, but One who has been tempted in all things as we are, yet without sin* (Hebrews 4:15). *He poured out Himself to death, and was numbered with the transgressors* (Isaiah 53:12). Jesus was the spotless Lamb of God with no sin. But He took all our sins and wrongdoings on himself when He took that walk to Calvary and allowed himself to be crucified.

Christ submitted himself to God's will, which He demonstrated by His willingness to be slain. If He was truly human, as we believe, do you think He wanted to die a cruel death of crucifixion? No one would want to do that. *He . . . began to be very distressed and troubled. And He said to them, "My soul is deeply grieved to the point of death; remain here and keep watch." And He went a little beyond them, and fell to the ground and began to pray that if it were possible, the hour might pass Him by. And He was saying, "Abba! Father! All things are possible for You; remove this cup from Me; yet not what I will, but what You will"* (Mark 14:33-36). Christ was willing to submit to God's will, no matter how difficult. In His case it was the worst possibility: a humiliating and painful death.

Pain is inevitable. But after one is slain in pain, then comes the joy! When Mary Magdalene and the other Mary came to the tomb in which Jesus had been laid, they met an angel who told them He was alive, for He had risen from the dead. We are told *they left the tomb quickly with fear and great joy* (Matthew 28:8). The resurrected Christ appeared to a group in Luke 24 and spoke to them. Luke 24:41 tells us, *While they still could not believe it because of their joy and amazement, He said to them, "Have you anything here to eat?"* After the ascension, *They . . . returned to Jerusalem with great joy, and were continually in the temple praising God* (verses 52-53).

So Christ was slain by
    humbling himself
    taking on the sin He did not deserve
    submitting himself to God's will
    experiencing pain
    and then receiving joy

We, too, are slain to anything but our relationship with God when we go through these same steps. Paul said, *I have been crucified with Christ; and it is no longer I who live, but Christ lives in me* (Galatians 2:20). These steps are what this passage means. Go back through the five steps as a conclusion to today's study and prayerfully ask the Father if you have been slain for God.

MEMORY CHALLENGE

Record Isaiah 40:31, which relates to Psalm 103:5.

Sang a New Song

Read Revelation 5:9-10.

1. If you have access to the *New International Version* translation of the Bible, record the first 10 words of Isaiah 5:1. If you don't have that translation, use another, recording the first phrase of that verse.

2. Record the first phrase of Revelation 5:9.

3. What was the song about? (Hint: Hebrews 9:11-12.)

4. Why was the song new at this time?

5. Record the following scriptures about our new song.

   Psalm 40:3

   Psalm 98:1

   Psalm 149:1

   Isaiah 42:10

6. Summarize Ecclesiastes 1:10.

This week we've seen how Revelation 5 progresses through God's plan for humanity. We recognize that we're all born in sin and need a Savior. The Savior had to be slain as a blood sacrifice in order to be our Redeemer. But since He was slain, we now have an opportunity to sing a new song.

The "new song" is actually an old song. It's the song of acclamation that God is in control of this world and that His plan of salvation and redemption can be stopped by no one. Christ will overcome evil and reign as Savior of the universe. The song is new in verse 9 because these things have now been accomplished. This is no longer a prophecy or a future event. The events described in the song have taken place, and the cast is not singing in faith but in praise of God's accomplishments. The song is also new because the Lamb will now take His rightful place on earth. He will reign instead of allowing Satan this privilege with humanity.

God gives us a new song when we become His children. *If anyone is in Christ, he is a new creature; the old things passed away; behold, new things have come* (2 Corinthians 5:17). The Holy Spirit changes us when we accept Jesus as our Savior. He gives us new desires, attitudes, ideas, understanding, goals, and mission statements. We are different. We will still be tempted by evil, but we will have a power to resist that we never had before and a desire to truly turn from it. Our hearts will be changed to want godliness and righteousness. We will entertain a love for others that we never felt before. *I will give you a new heart and put a new spirit within you; and I will remove the heart of stone from your flesh and give you a heart of flesh* (Ezekiel 36:26). Our song will no longer be off-key. We may hit a wrong note now and then, but for the most part, our song will be strong, melodious, and beautiful.

The four living creatures and elders in Revelation 5 were singing about the worthiness of God and the Lamb. The song had a new meaning because it was the song of the redeemed. The Lamb's credentials were disclosed to the world. He had been slain, and with His blood, every man and woman from every nation and race was purchased for God. There would now be a kingdom that would reign on earth with a community of priests to serve. They would sing eternally. *I will sing of the lovingkindness of the LORD forever* (Psalm 89:1).

MEMORY CHALLENGE

How are our years satisfied? How is our youth renewed?

Saying Honor and Glory

Read Revelation 5:11-12.

1. How many angels, living creatures, and elders are mentioned in verse 11?

2. These numbers were prophesied in Daniel. Record Daniel 7:10.

3. Look back to yesterday's lesson and question 5. Reread the scriptures you recorded, and look for the action word contained in three of them (other than "sang"). What is it?

4. What was the sevenfold praise they gave the Lamb (Revelation 5:12)?

5. Write out some ideas that you learn from the following scriptures regarding honor and glory.

   John 1:14

   2 Corinthians 4:6

   2 Peter 1:17

6. Record 1 Timothy 1:17.

By human nature, we love to receive honor and glory. If we were to be named Employee of the Year or Mother of the Year, we would cherish the award. What a tribute to our hard work, intelligence, and ingenuity! Even small compliments about a good Sunday School lesson or a beautiful solo give us an opportunity to take credit for what we have accomplished. Humanly we can accept those honors, but as Christians, we are to give the honor and glory to God.

I remember when Vonda Kay Van Dyke was crowned Miss America. While I do not remember her exact words, I do remember that when she accepted the honor, she gave God the credit. She praised Him and admitted that all that happened to her was His doing.

In other situations, I've seen a sports figure be the hero of the game by making a big interception, hitting a home run, or sinking a timely basket. In the postgame interview, the announcer will ask something like, "What were you thinking when you saw the ball in the air?" More than once, a player will begin by giving God the glory by responding with something like this: "I just want to thank God for the abilities He's given me as an athlete and the opportunity today to be in the right place at the right time." How often does the announcer skip right over that, almost being irritated that the player had to throw it in? It's as though the announcer is saying, "Let's get to the important stuff."

Giving God the honor and glory *is* the important stuff.

God will share His glory with no one but His Son, Jesus Christ. Everything He enables us to do is because of His power, gifts, insight, love, courage, and strength within us. Without Him we can do nothing. When we take the glory ourselves, we actually steal it from God. He is due all honor and glory.

Someday *myriads upon myriads* will put God and His Son in the proper place and say in a loud voice, *Worthy is the Lamb.* Only He should receive the *power and riches and wisdom and might and honor and glory and blessing.* On that day not one of us will share the glory with God. What a great time—now—to begin practicing!

MEMORY CHALLENGE

Fill in the blanks:

Who _____ your years with _____

_____, so that your _____ is _____

like the _____.

                                                        Psalm 103:5

Sovereign

Read Revelation 5:13-14.

1. Who said, *To Him who sits on the throne, and to the Lamb, be blessing and honor and glory and dominion forever and ever?*

2. Read Philippians 2:9-11. Will there be a time that even atheists, backsliders, demons, and blasphemers will admit that Jesus Christ really is the world's Savior?

3. Define the word "sovereign," using a dictionary or a Bible concordance.

4. Summarize the following verses, which speak of the sovereignty of God.

   Deuteronomy 4:39

   1 Chronicles 29:12

   Isaiah 44:24

   Isaiah 45:5

   1 Timothy 6:15-16

5. You have written a definition and built on it with scriptures. If you were asked to explain to a nonbeliever the sovereignty of God, how would you describe it?

The fifth chapter of Revelation is summed up by the fact that God has supreme power and control over what happens on earth and under the earth and in heaven. Humanity may believe that they have influence or power to control their own destinies or those of others, but in reality only God has that power.

How many times in the Bible have we read stories of a person or people who thought they had the power? For a while they appeared to be right, but when God was ready, He always took charge and showed them He was really in control. Remember Belshazzar, the king in Daniel 5? He held a big feast and ordered the gold and silver vessels that his father, Nebuchadnezzar, had taken from the Temple in Jerusalem to be used for drinking toasts to the idols. Belshazzar was on a roll; he was the king of the mountain. He was filled with arrogance and belief that he had the world at his feet and could do anything he wanted. Daniel 5:5-6 reads, *Suddenly the fingers of man's hand emerged and began writing opposite the lampstand on the plaster of the wall of the king's palace, and the king saw the back of the hand that did the writing. Then the king's face grew pale, and his thoughts alarmed him; and his hip joints went slack, and his knees began knocking together.*

Suddenly and without warning, something happened out of Belshazzar's control that immediately put him in his place before God. When confronted with that reality, the king was overcome with fear. He called for someone to interpret the message written by the hand, and Daniel entered the scene. Don't miss the excitement—turn now to Daniel 5:13-30 and read the rest of the story.

This is just one of many examples God gives us of someone who foolishly thought he or she had power only to realize too late that it was an attempt to steal God's sovereignty. That is how Revelation 5 concludes. We are told that *every created thing* everywhere will admit that only God is worthy of blessing, honor, glory, and dominion. There will be no holdouts. All those who are so sure they have power will be reduced to confession that Jesus Christ is Lord and is in control.

God is sovereign. Nothing humanity does or claims can change that. Let's not wait for the day we're forced to admit this truth. Let's admit it now and live our lives in accordance with its truth.

Written by Linda Shaw

Write by memory the scripture for this week.

Revelation

LESSON 6

■ **A Study of Revelation 6**

Seal One Is Broken

Read Revelation 6:1-11 aloud.

1. In Revelation 6:1, what did John see?

2. Describe the Lamb (Revelation 5:6).

3. In Revelation 6:1, what did John hear?

4. Describe the living creatures mentioned in Revelation 4:8.

5. Describe what happened after one of the creatures said, *Come* (Revelation 6:2).

6. Summarize briefly the warnings given in these verses.

   Matthew 24:4-5

   Matthew 24:24

   2 Thessalonians 2:3

   1 John 2:22

2 John 1:7

There are three principal series of judgments in Revelation—the seal judgments, the trumpet judgments, and the bowl judgments. The Lamb opens the seals, angels sound the trumpets, and God himself pours out the bowls of His wrath.

Under the seal judgments, humanity ruins the world. Events recorded under the seals are extensions of things happening in our world today.

Under the trumpet judgments, Satan rules the world. A greater dimension of the supernatural comes upon the earth. Satan is cast down to earth along with hordes of evil spirits; Satan's plans for this earth are fulfilled.

Under the bowl judgments, God rescues the world. His wrath is revealed from heaven, He deals Satan's empire blow after blow until at last He puts an end to this world's woes.

As the Lamb breaks the first seal, John hears a noise like thunder. This thunder speaks of a coming storm, even though everything seems peaceful. At the command of one of the living creatures, a warrior comes forth on a white horse with a bow in his hand. A bow signifies a distant victorious war. No mention is made of arrows, which would indicate a bloodless victory. He receives the crown of a victor, but it is not the crown of a sovereign ruler.

MEMORY CHALLENGE

Psalm 103:6

The LORD performs righteous deeds and judgments for all who are oppressed.

In chapter 6 we are looking at the beginning of the judgments of God, and in chapter 19 we see the end of them. There is much dispute as to what the rider on the white horse represents. Some identify him as Jesus, because in Revelation 19 Jesus appears on a white horse, wearing a crown, and brings to an end all the terrible series of judgments that have come upon the earth. But this could be mistaken identification, because the context is entirely different.

But it is significant that this rider on the white horse bears some resemblance to the appearance of Jesus in chapter 19. They both wear crowns, and both are going out to conquer. It suggests that this rider is someone who is like Christ but is not Christ. Through the Bible—in the Old Testament and New Testament—biblical prophecies tell us about the Antichrist. They remind us that one day there will come a world leader of such irresistible magnitude that the world will be swept off its feet. He will charm the public, deceive the nations, and control the planet. The majority of Bible scholars believe the man on the white horse in Revelation 6 is the Antichrist. He is Satan's masterpiece and the counterfeit of all that Christ is or claims to be. He will be the master of deceit. He plans to deceive you.

Today many good people are being deceived. The New Age movement has become a powerful force in Satan's strategy to blind the world to the truth of the gospel of Jesus Christ. It claims that men and women have secret powers or hidden abilities within that, if discovered, will enable them to rule and manipulate people and run our world to suit ourselves. These ideas are constantly being fed into the human mind through television, movies, videos, and magazines. New Agers want to help you "find yourself" by finding their concept of God—"All is God. God is all. Man is part of all; therefore, man is God."

Almost every aspect of New Age teaching counterfeits the truth of the gospel of Jesus Christ. However, just as we don't quit using real currency because someone has made counterfeit currency, we must not abandon a single truth of the gospel. If there is counterfeit money circulating, we must become more familiar with what's real so that we'll be able to recognize what's false. We must do the same with the essential truths of the gospel that the enemy is trying to steal. He would not be after these truths if they were not important.

There are many other false doctrines that are deceiving well-intentioned people. In 1 Timothy 4:1-2 we are warned, *The Spirit explicitly says that in later times some will fall away from the faith, paying attention to deceitful spirits and doctrines of demons, by means of the hypocrisy of liars.* David Koresh claimed to be Jesus Christ and convinced his followers that he was the only person who could correctly interpret the seven seals in Revelation. Opening the seals, he said, proved that he was the Lamb of God, Jesus Christ in the flesh. A typically self-deceived extremist cult leader, Koresh perished with near-

ly 90 of his followers in the flames of Ranch Apocalypse near Waco, Texas, in 1993. Many deceived people died believing lies. Pride and arrogance are the sins that can lead a person to become spiritually deceived. Satan lures us into spiritual darkness by telling us that we have found the real truth and that everybody else is wrong.

How can we combat the darkness and the blasphemous lies taught by false doctrines? The solution is not to ignore them, but to take our stand on the truth and bring His light into their darkness. After all, light is more powerful than darkness. When we open our shades or drapes at night, darkness does not come into our rooms—rather, light shines out into the darkness. We need not fear Satan's deception if we know the Light, Jesus.

All false teachers distort the Word of God and the Person and work of Jesus Christ. As such, they oppose Christ in the same way (though not with the same intensity) as will the Antichrist. In the same sense that John the Baptist was a forerunner of Jesus Christ, so are these false teachers forerunners of the Antichrist.

The rider on the white horse is the revelation that the worst is yet to come. Today we are living amid great deceit, but it's not as bad as it's going to be. There is coming an even greater lie. God is allowing peace to be taken from the earth (6:4), and this allows deceit to have its way with people until it reaches the point of delusion.

Briefly summarize 2 Thessalonians 2:9-12.

Dear Lord, help us to test every spirit that tries to deceive us. We want only Your truths—they are our only protection.

Seal Two Is Broken

Read Revelation 6:3-4.

1. After the Lamb had broken the second seal, what did John hear?

2. What did John see?

3. What authority was granted to the rider of the red horse?

4. What was given to the rider?

5. With the breaking of the second seal, universal war breaks out and peace is banished from the earth. Record a scripture that's comforting to you when you struggle to keep peace in your own life.

The second seal is opened. This rider on the fiery red horse is easier to recognize. With his power to remove peace from the earth and to make people slay each other, his name must be "war" and "bloodshed." In the beginning, this is not war between great armies. To slay is to slaughter—a reference to civil war, in which mobs of people gather together to attack and destroy others whom they dislike. We're seeing this every day as it happens in some third-world nations. In the United States, gang wars have raged in the streets in our largest cities and other places. It is a murderous slaying of citizens by people unrestrained by any self-control. The peace of the earth is being removed as Jesus Christ has been taken out of authority in vital areas of our world.

Eventually we will encounter "the large sword." In the days when John wrote, there were no megabombs, missiles, tanks, or any of the modern weapons of warfare. Such weapons of destruction had to be put in terms that people would understand in that day. The major weapon of destruction at that time was a sword. This was a "large sword," a powerful weapon of destruction. In today's world, most commentators see this as a picture of the awesome power of a nuclear bomb or biological warfare in mammoth proportions, something that destroys enormous numbers of people. If you choose to do further reading, in Ezekiel 38 and 39 you'll find a vivid description of such warfare, in which armies come out of the North into the Holy Land and are destroyed by what appears to be radiation or biological sickness.[1]

6. What are your thoughts as you consider your future?

Believers today live in a world where evil is rampant and often seems out of control. We are confronted daily with headlines of war, tragedy, catastrophe, and inhumanity. Prophetic teaching tells us that although God is still on the throne, He is allowing evil to run its course. However, this will not always be the case. Just as the focus of redemption revolves around the person and work of Jesus Christ, we will see the focus of human evil revolve around the person and work of the Antichrist. While it may be near, knowing God's plan in advance gives us as Christians confidence that God will triumph over evil—even the greatest concentration of evil in the Antichrist.

7. Ask God to show you how to help a non-Christian friend or family member see his or her need for Christ.

Thank You, Father, for peace that passes all human understanding as we study times of war and upheaval in the future.

Fill in the blanks:

The LORD _____ righteous deeds and judgments for all who are _____.

                                                        Psalm 103:6

Seal Three Is Broken

Read Revelation 6:5-6.

1. After the Lamb had broken the third seal, what did John see?

2. From where did the voice come?

3. What did the voice from near the throne of God declare?

4. What does God want us to do as we wait for Him to judge the earth?

5. Pray for someone who reacts negatively to the message of Christ.

6. Are you being accountable to someone to help you memorize scripture?

The first two horsemen are sent out as champion warriors. They both bear weapons of warfare—the first rider held a bow and the second a large sword. The first, who rides a white horse, wears the crown, the symbol of military conquest. The second, who rides a red horse, is intent upon engaging the enemy in battle. God has given earth over to itself to engage in a global, civil war, preventing its inhabitants from attaining the very things that make for their peace and security.

Romans 1:28 tells us, *So it was that when they gave God up and would not even acknowledge him, God gave them up to doing everything their evil minds could think of* (TLB).

Together the horsemen take peace from the earth; these symbols of military strife call attention to a fallen creation, which now exists under the curse of God.

The third horseman, riding a black horse, is sent out by the third living creature holding a pair of scales in his hand. John here envisions a "siege economy." Creation's civil war results in a scarcity of the staples necessary to sustain human life, and the rapid inflation prices make it impossible for the poor to survive. The scales of the third horseman measure the economic structures of a fallen world—the runaway inflation of an economy in ruins, in which money is worthless and food must be rationed.

One day's wages will buy enough food for one person's physical needs. There would be nothing for their family. But the luxuries, the oil and the wine, are left untouched. Does this imply that during these evil times there will be an abundant supply of oil and wine, but the people will suffer greatly from a lack of bread? With wheat, barley, oil, and wine being staple foods of both Palestine and Asia Minor, these conditions become an excuse for the rigid controls over buying and selling that we find in chapter 13 when, under the reign of Antichrist, the whole world is subjected to enormously restrictive controls so that no one can buy or sell without the mark of the beast (Revelation 13:17).[1]

Dear Father, with unthinkable inflation, economics out of control, and panic in the marketplace, let us be in the shelter of Your presence. Yea, though we walk through the valley of the shadow of death, we fear no evil, for You are with us."

MEMORY CHALLENGE

Fill in the blanks:

The LORD performs _____ _____ and _____ for all who are _____.

Psalm 103:6

Seal Four Is Broken

Read Revelation 6:7-8.

When the Lamb broke the fourth seal, John heard the voice of the fourth living creature saying, *Come.* When he looked, he saw the fourth horse.

1. What was the color of the horse and the name of the rider?

2. Who followed the horse and the rider?

3. How much of the earth were they given authority over?

4. What four ways were they allowed to kill in this portion of the earth?

5. Summarize similar prophecy against Jerusalem in Ezekiel 5:16-17.

The seals of the scroll are broken one by one. Restraint is increasingly removed from the earth. When the first seal is broken and blasphemous philosophies are sent forth to subdue the earth, they will race around the world with unbelievable speed. With the breaking of the second seal, we know that God once sent humanity an offer of peace when the Prince of Peace was born, but they scorned and crucified Him. Until He comes back in power, war must go on until at last war itself is personified, mounted on a blood-red horse, and sent forth with a great sword to summon men to the terrible wars of the Apocalypse. Economic disaster follows the breaking of the third seal. When the rider of the black horse comes, he will control the economy of starving humanity and will wipe them out by the millions.

For the last time, John is summoned to *Come.* When the fourth seal is broken, John sees a horse the color of death. Its rider is named Death, and Hades is following close behind him. With the power given to them, they will kill by sword, famine, pestilence, and wild beasts. They are limited to one-fourth of the earth.

War and famine will continue to plague humanity. God created the world as a good environment that would normally provide ample water and food for humanity (Genesis 1). However, the productivity of the earth is related to people's obedience to God. For example, the sins of Adam, Eve, and Cain resulted in the unfruitfulness of the earth (3:17-18). Israel's relationship with God also directly affected the fertility of the Promised Land. When the people obeyed God, the land was productive (Deuteronomy 11:11-14). However, when they disobeyed, judgment came on the land by drought and famine (11:16-17). When God did send drought and famine on His people, it was for the purpose of bringing them to repentance (Amos 4:6-8). And in Revelation 6:8 and Matthew 24:7 we see that famine is a part of God's coming judgment of the earth in the last days.

Added to war and famine is pestilence. Pestilence is defined as a devastating epidemic of diseases. War and famine invariably give rise to pestilence. Or could this refer to biological warfare, the willful spreading of diseases among masses of people so that they're destroyed?

Could it be possible that wild beasts of the earth multiply and humans become subject to attacks by these predators? In these end times, will ferocious animals begin preying on the world's people?

In a recent article published in the *Sunday Oklahoman,* a tragic incident was reported from Issaquah, Washington. It caused me to see the possibility that wild beasts could kill people as described in Revelation 6:8.

> The typical cougar is a shy creature that avoids people and prefers to eat deer rather than pets or children. So much for typical. Two children watched from the doorway of their home as a cougar chased and killed their Labrador dog. When the state game warden and a hunter arrived with two hounds, this cougar had no intention of fleeing. The hounds came across it just 100 yards into the woods. The snarling cougar turned on the dogs with a fury that sent them both back wounded. Forty minutes later two other hunters and two fresh hounds returned, thinking the cougar would have headed for the dense woods. Instead, they found it just a few hundred feet away. They shot and killed the 145-pound male cougar. . . .

> "I've had dealings with upward of 100 mountain lions, and that was the most aggressive I've seen," said the state game warden. "This cougar wasn't sick or injured. It obviously didn't concern him to be around people, and dogs were just for lunch." . . .

Of the 10 fatal cougar attacks on people recorded since 1890 in the United States, half were in the past 10 years. Nonfatal attacks are also on the rise, as are reports of cougars preying on pets and livestock. . . .

This year, cougars have been spotted lounging on a porch in Villa Park, California, munching house cats near Kalispell, Montana, and wandering by an elementary school in Reno, Nevada. In each case, the cougar was shot by officials fearing further problems.[1]

In addition to the attack of cougars in the West, there was an attack by a coyote in the East, in Boston. State wildlife officials say they can't figure out why the animal attacked a toddler on Cape Cod, the first documented case in Massachusetts. There have been only a handful of cases nationwide. Lab results indicate that the coyote did not have distemper, mange, rabies, or any other disease that might prompt an animal to attack a human. Investigators also talked to neighbors but found no evidence that someone had been feeding or caring for the coyote.

Matthew 8:32 records that Jesus found a legion of demons in one man and allowed them to enter into pigs when they left the man. Will it be possible for Satan through the Antichrist to demon-possess animals for the destruction prophesied in this chapter?

Four seals of the seven-sealed scroll have been broken at this point in Revelation. These four seal-judgments are all extensions of forces that are already at work among us, but they will be carried to an unprecedented extreme in that day. These four seals confirm God's recorded method of making people face up to the truth that they're refusing to admit their sin.

It is important to see that the four horsemen are under command and not themselves in full control. In fact, it is the Lamb who is opening the seals and so is truly in control of all that is taking place. It is by His will, or at least by His permission, that the horsemen ride.

If the forces of the four seal-judgments are already working among us, we should pray Psalm 139:23-24: *Search me, O God, and know my heart; try me and know my anxious thoughts; and see if there be any hurtful way in me, and lead me in the everlasting way.*

Are we being deceived and wanting to believe lies? Are we seeking to kill or destroy someone's reputation? Are we simplifying our lives to eliminate extravagance? Is there a famine of reading and obeying God's Word in our homes? Are we demanding power and control rather being willing to submit to one another?

Help us, dear Father, to recognize the spirit of the Antichrist where he has determined to deceive and destroy us.

Bless the LORD, *O* _____ _____, *and all that is* _____ *me, bless His* _____ _____. *Bless the* LORD, *O my soul, and* _____ *none of His* _____; *who pardons all your* _____; *who* _____ *all your diseases; who* _____ *your life from the* _____, *who crowns you with lovingkindness and* _____; *who satisfies your years with* _____ _____, *so that your youth is renewed like the* _____. *The* LORD *performs righteous deeds and* _____ *for all who are oppressed.*

Psalm 103:1-6

DAY FIVE

Seal Five Is Broken

Read Revelation 6:9-11.

1. After the Lamb had broken the fifth seal, what did John see underneath the altar?

2. Why had they been slain?

3. What were they wanting from the Lord?

4. What was given to each of them?

5. Why were they to rest for a little longer?

6. Hebrews 11:36-38 gives us a picture of what persecuted Christians in parts of the world must endure today. Briefly summarize this passage.

7. Do you know of a faithful Christian today who is being persecuted for following Christ? Share with your group if time allows. Think of ways you could encourage that person.

How people can die over the course of a period of time and yet all arrive in heaven together is a phenomenon that marks the difference between time and eternity.

John is seeing the great Temple in heaven, which Moses saw when he was on Mount Sinai (Exodus 26:30). The Tabernacle contained a great brazen altar and a laver in the outer court. The martyrs are seen *under the altar* because that's where the blood was placed (Leviticus 17:11).

In Revelation 6:10, the prayer of the martyrs is a call for vengeance. This is quite different from the prayer Christians are expected to pray for their enemies. When Stephen, the first Christian martyr, saw the Lord as he was being stoned, he said to Him, *Lord, do not hold this sin against them!* (Acts 7:60). He was asking that his murderers be forgiven, for they did not know what they were doing. This is the prayer of believers today for those who persecute us or take unfair advantage of us. The martyrs in Revelation 6:10 pray not for personal vengeance but for God's glorification and vindication. And they are not living in days when God patiently endures the injustices of men. These are days of judgment—when wrongdoers are being called to account for their actions. The prayers, then, of God's people reflect the mind of God at that time. Led by the Spirit, they pray for what God intends to do during the Last Days.

Jim Elliot, a missionary who gave his life as a martyr in the jungles of Ecuador, wrote, "He is no fool who loses what he cannot keep to gain what he cannot lose."

When German theologian Dietrich Bonhoeffer went to his death at the hand of the Nazis, his last words were "O God, this is the end; but for me it is just the beginning."

In the December 6, 1993, issue of the *New Yorker*, reporter Mark Danner described the army's reaction to a Christian girl from El Mozote, El Salvador:

> There was one in particular the soldiers talked about that evening (she is mentioned in the Tutela legal report as well): a girl on La Cruz whom they had raped many times during the course of the afternoon, and through it all, while the other women of El Mozote had screamed and cried as if they had never had a man, this girl had sung hymns, strange evangelical songs, and she kept right on singing, too, even after they had done what had to be done, and shot her in the chest. . . .
>
> She had lain there on La Cruz with blood flowing from her chest, and had kept on singing—a bit weaker than before, but still singing. And the soldiers, stupefied, had watched and pointed. Then they had grown tired of the game and shot her again, and she sang still, and their wonder began to turn to fear—until finally they had unsheathed their machetes and hacked through her neck, and at last the singing stopped.

Please pray for Christians who are being persecuted and especially for those who are destined to be martyred and will join those *under the altar.*

MEMORY CHALLENGE

What does the Lord do for all who are oppressed?

Recite Psalm 103:6 five times.

Seal Six Is Broken

Read Revelation 6:12-17.

1. From verses 12-14, list six reactions of nature to the opening of the sixth seal.

2. In verse 15, how did the inhabitants of earth respond to the events unleashed by the breaking of the seals?

3. Name the classes of people mentioned.

4. How will people try to escape being judged by God?

5. What is a natural disaster (earthquake, tornado, flood, or other) that stands out in your memory?

6. Can you imagine crying out to be killed during a disaster?

Following the breaking of the sixth seal there is total chaos on earth. People are absolutely horrified at what they see. This is the picture of the absolute panic of the last days. People's hearts are now failing with fear as they look at what is coming on the earth. They feel that the day of wrath has finally come. In this they are wrong, for these things are only *the beginning of sorrows* (Matthew 24:8, KJV).

The disasters described here can, of course, be taken literally. Drastic changes in the heavens could result in earthquakes and devastating changes in the topography of the planet. It's also possible that the description is symbolic and depicts total collapse of the establishment. The earth-quake suggests that everything stable in society will be shaken. The disasters of the sun, the moon, and stars suggest the downfall or the plunging into confusion of all the governing bodies. The moving of the islands and the mountains indicates tremendous changes in constituted government.

Complete panic is described next. It affects every class of society from the lowest slave to the highest king. In relation to judgment from the Lord Jesus Christ, everyone is in the same predicament. Success in the world doesn't help; no one escapes. The Book of Revelation discredits those who hold that God is so loving and kind that He'll never judge people who have not received His Son. Though modern humanity is reluctant to accept the fact that God will judge the wicked, the Bible clearly teaches that He will. The Scriptures certainly reveal a God of love; however, they also reveal a God of wrath who will deal with those who refuse the grace offered in the Lord Jesus Christ.

In that day, those who refuse to believe have reached a stage at which they cannot believe. They do not repent and pray to the Lord for salvation. Rather, they feel a terrible fear and pray to the rocks to destroy them. They will manifest openly and publicly what they feel privately and secretly today. It is a strange phenomenon, but it is easily confirmed—that every unbeliever is convinced in his or her heart that death is somehow an escape into oblivion. They think they can escape the terrible consequences of their evil by dying. But the Word of God assures us that this is not true: *It is appointed unto men once to die, but after this the judgment* (Hebrews 9:27, KJV).

An unknown writer has written, "God's wrath is God's love dammed up by man's disobedience, until it has to be poured out in righteous judgment."

Who is able to stand? (Revelation 6:17). The answer is obvious: Only those who avail themselves to the grace of God, even though they suffer a martyr's death in this future tragic period.

Dear loving Father, show us someone today whom we can help accept Your saving grace. We want this person to be ready.

Written by Marie Coody

MEMORY CHALLENGE

Quote Psalm 103:1-6 to someone in your discussion group.

Revelation

LESSON 7

■ A Study of Revelation 7

DAY ONE

Call Waiting

Read all of Revelation 7 aloud.
Review Revelation 7:1-3.

We have seen six of the seven seals opened, but before the seventh seal is broken, God is calling for a time of waiting.

1. After the judgments of chapter 6, John sees four angels. Where are they standing?

2. What are the angels doing? Why?

3. What did John see coming from the east?

4. What did the angel from the east have in his possession?

5. What power or authority did the four angels possess?

6. When were the angels given permission to harm the earth and the sea?

The breaking of the sixth seal left us with the vision of the earth in shattering upheaval. All that is on the earth and in the sky is in turmoil. How will anyone be able to survive? Then in chapter 7 we learn of an unexpected time of waiting before the last seal is broken. A holy restraint is placed upon the terrors of the four horsemen. Four angels, who are active in the trumpet judgments and who hold in their hands further tempests of fury, are restrained by a decree of God.

A stillness will descend on human affairs. The world's politicians will no doubt pride themselves that their diplomacy and astuteness have brought about this tranquillity. The sudden peace, however, will be none of humanity's doing, but God's. In reality, it is simply a lull between storms. This call to wait is so that 144,000 of God's people can be sealed.

Waiting is sometimes a part of God's plan for believers. One of the greatest spiritual disciplines of our lives is the time of waiting on God. Scriptures help us understand God's purposes for it.

Record the phrases from the following scriptures that relate to waiting.

Why should we wait on God?
   Psalm 25:1-2

   Psalm 27:14

   Psalm 33:20

   Psalm 37:9

   Psalm 62:1

   Psalm 123:2

   Habakkuk 2:2-3

MEMORY CHALLENGE

Psalm 103:7

He made known His ways to Moses,
His acts to the sons of Israel.

How should we wait on God?
>   Psalm 25:5
>
>   Psalm 37:7
>
>   Psalm 59:1-3, 16-17
>
>   Psalm 62:5
>
>   Psalm 130:5
>
>   Lamentations 3:26
>
>   Hosea 12:6
>
>   Micah 7:7

What results from waiting on God?
>   Psalm 25:3
>
>   Psalm 37:9
>
>   Psalm 40:1
>
>   Isaiah 25:9
>
>   Isaiah 30:18
>
>   Isaiah 40:31
>
>   Isaiah 64:4
>
>   Lamentations 3:25

God may seem slow to us as we wait, but He tells us that a thousand years are but as yesterday to Him (Psalm 90:4). He simply is not on our timetable. He gives us opportunities to develop Christlike character.

As John continues revealing his dream in Revelation 7, the implication is that the judgment of God is impending, but before its infliction on earth, God wants to set apart and protect His servants. God places His Great Seal on His followers, identifying them as His own and guaranteeing His protection over their souls. This shows how valuable we are to Him. Our physical bodies may be beaten, maimed, or even destroyed, but nothing can harm the souls of those marked by God.

DAY TWO

His Seal of Protection

Read Revelation 7:3-8.

1. What people were to receive a seal?

2. Where were they to receive the seal?

3. How many individuals in John's vision were sealed?

4. How many were sealed from each of the 12 tribes of Israel?

An angel of God said to delinquent Lot, *I can do nothing until you are there* (Genesis 19:22, TLB). When God sent the Flood upon the earth, He separated Noah and his family from the rest of the human race, and the Flood did not hurt them (6—8). When God destroyed Jericho, He protected Rahab and her household. Wicked though she was, she had put her trust in God, and God protected her from the judgment that fell on Jericho (Joshua 6:17-25). Just so, God will not allow the Great Tribulation to develop until He has secured and sealed a remnant of believing Jews from the tribes of Israel.

The tribe of Judah occupied the strategically important territory just west of the Dead Sea. The city of Jerusalem was on the border between Judah and Benjamin. David was from the tribe of Judah.

The tribe of Reuben inherited the territory just east of the Dead Sea; this was the first parcel of land to be bestowed. This region was well adapted for flocks and herds and was a tableland quite capable of cultivation.

The tribe of Gad's territory was the east side of the Jordan

River and the Dead Sea. The men of Gad achieved great expertise as warriors.

The tribe of Asher occupied the region along the northern coastal region of Palestine on the Mediterranean Sea. Perhaps Asher's greatest hero was Anna, the prophet who bore witness to the baby Jesus (Luke 2:36-38).

The tribe of Naphtali inhabited an area north of the Sea of Galilee that extends along the northwest side of the Jordan River. The territory finally succumbed to Tiglath-pileser III in 734 B.C.

Half of the tribe of Manasseh settled on the east bank of the Jordan and half on the west. Gideon is the most familiar of the descendents of Manasseh. He defeated the Midianites with a small band of men (Judges 6—7).

Simeon's inheritance lay within the inheritance of the tribe of Judah (Joshua 19:1) in the southern Negev. The tribe of Simeon seemed to be characterized by weakness.

The tribe of Levi became the landless priestly tribe. They were not given a tribal inheritance in the Promised Land (God was their inheritance) but were placed in 48 Levitical cities throughout the land. The tithe of the rest of the nation was used to provide for the needs of the Levites.

The tribe of Issachar occupied territory in the northern part of Palestine, just southwest of the Sea of Galilee. This tribe was not prominent in Israel's history.

The tribe of Zebulun settled in the area between the Sea of Galilee and Mount Carmel. This tribe hosted the other tribes with religious festivals at Mount Tabor. Their menu included delicacies fished from the Sea of Galilee. Militarily, the tribe distinguished itself in the struggles to possess the land, fighting faithfully in the armies of Deborah, Barak, and Gideon.

Two of the tribes of Israel came from Joseph: Ephraim and Manasseh. Jacob adopted them, and therefore they each became the father of a tribe of Israel.

The tribe of Benjamin occupied the smallest territory of all the tribes, being assigned the district lying between those of Judah and Ephraim. Benjamin played a significant role in Israelite history. Saul, Israel's first king, was a Benjamite. In the New Testament, the apostle Paul proudly proclaimed his heritage in the tribe of Benjamin.

Why is the tribe of Dan omitted? It was suggested in several commentaries that Dan was left out because this was the first tribe to go into idolatry (Judges 18). Early rabbinical writings emphasize the apostasy of Dan. Other writers claim that Dan was omitted because the Antichrist will come from this tribe. They use the scripture Jeremiah 8:16 for the basis of their theory.

5. Record Jeremiah 8:16, considering this thought.

Those sealed will go unscathed through the great Tribulation. They will be a perpetual thorn in the side of the beast and a constant reminder to the devil that, while millions may bow to his will, God still has him on a leash and says to him, "This far and no farther." The mobilized armies of the earth will not be able to touch a hair on the heads of the sealed ones. The concentration camps and torture chambers of the beast's fearful inquisition will leave them unscathed. The fire will not kindle upon them, nor will the smell of smoke be on their garments. The floods will not drown them. The secret police will have documents as thick as prison walls, but they will be unable to harm them. The seal of God rests upon them, and they are saved and secured. They will be a living proof to the devil that not only is his secular power strictly limited by divine decree, but in the end, he cannot win. If he cannot conquer these, then he cannot possibly win in the end. No matter how many millions he liquidates in his insane rage, he is obviously under God's control.

The 144,000 are sealed to defy the totality of Satan's secular dominion. They are a reminder to him that not every knee bows to him and that God is sovereign and in invincible control.

The seal on the forehead is equivalent to the divine mark of ownership that elsewhere in the New Testament is referred to as the presence of the Holy Spirit (2 Corinthians 1:22; Ephesians 1:13; 4:30). This act of God will fulfill the promise of the Philadelphian church: *Since you have kept my command to endure patiently, I will also keep you from the hour of trial that is going to come upon the whole world to test those who live on the earth* (Revelation 3:10, NIV).

The description of the judgments under the sixth seal ends with the question, *The great day of their wrath has come, and who is able to stand?* (6:17). Chapter 7 answers this question by implying that only the true servants of God, who are divinely sealed, can be protected from the wrath of God and the Lamb.

6. Briefly summarize the following scriptures.

Every Christian is—
born of the Spirit (John 3:5-6)

gifted with the Spirit (Acts 2:38)

indwelled by the Spirit (1 Corinthians 6:19)

marked with His seal, the Holy Spirit (Ephesians 1:13)

The Holy Spirit is the common experience of every Christian's life. He identifies the Christian as surely as if His name were marked upon each forehead. The Holy Spirit is the mark and the seal of the Christian.

MEMORY CHALLENGE

Fill in the blanks:

He made known His ways to _____,

His acts to the sons of _____.

Psalm 103:7

DAY THREE

Martyr? Who? Me?

Read Revelation 7:9.

1. Where was the great multitude standing?

2. Were they numbered?

3. Where were they from?

4. How were they dressed?

5. What was in their hands?

Chapter 7 of the Book of Revelation serves as a review of the situation described in the previous six chapters and emphasizes two important facts.

First, God is going to judge Israel in the period of the great trial, and 12,000 from each tribe, totaling 144,000, will be protected and sealed from the judgments that will fall upon the world in general.

Second, a great multitude of Gentiles will also be saved, but many of these will be martyred. A multitude of the martyred dead will be found in heaven rejoicing in the presence of the Lamb and representing every tongue and nation. This is an indication that even in the tragic closing hours prior to the second coming of Christ to the earth, countless souls will find Christ as Savior and be saved by His grace.

The *great multitude in heaven* is composed of all who remained faithful to God. They are in the innermost court. They are before the throne of God. They are dressed in white robes, which is symbolic of the fact that they have been set apart for God and made pure and sinless. Revelation 3:4 tells us that they are those *who have not soiled their garments; and they will walk with Me in white, for they are worthy.* Soiled garments represent turning from Christ through unbelief and worship of false gods.

Palm branches were in their hands (Revelation 7:9). Palm branches were emblems of victory. In Leviticus 23:40, Moses instructed the Israelites to *take . . . palm branches . . . and you shall rejoice before the LORD your God for seven days* during the Feast of Tabernacles. John 12:12-13 tells how the great multitude took palm branches to greet Jesus as He entered Jerusalem.

6. Summarize these passages.

   Romans 8:35-38

   Philippians 1:21

7. What in your life is worth being persecuted for?

   What in your life is worth dying for?

In a world in which life doesn't always go well and many people are constantly tempted to take the "easy way out," the mark of the true Christian is a long and hard obedience to God.

8. Do you know anyone personally who will be among the martyrs standing before Him on His throne? (Share this with your group.)

9. Look back to Revelation Lesson 4, Day 1. Do you believe God would have you assume responsibility to pray for those suffering religious persecution?

MEMORY CHALLENGE

When you hear the name "Moses," what do you remember about him?

DAY FOUR

Salvation Is for Everyone

Read Revelation 7:10.

1. Record Revelation 7:10.

The *Amplified Bible* translates the same verse in this way: *In loud voice they cried, saying, [Our] salvation is due to our God, Who is seated on the throne, and to the Lamb [to Them we owe our deliverance]!*

They are thanking God for the gift of salvation.

They are in heaven
   not because they were willing to be martyred,
   not because they had given their bodies to be burned,
   not because they had endured to the end,
   not because they took joyfully being stripped of all
      their belongings,
   not because they came through the Great Tribulation,
   but because of the Lamb.

Every martyr was praising God for salvation. All believers from every generation have met the single requirement that allows them to stand before God's throne in front of the Lamb in their white robes. Robes are whitened by the Lamb's blood. Life in Him must be purchased through His death. Our unsaved loved ones must know this in order for them to stand before the throne of a merciful God.

It is important for us as Christians to know the scriptures that will help unbelievers understand God's salvation. For years many have known the "Roman road to salvation." In the *Life Application Study Bible* it is now titled "Salvation's Freeway."

   Romans 3:23   Everyone has sinned.
   Romans 6:23   The penalty for our sin is death.
   Romans 5:8   Jesus Christ died for sin.
   Romans 10:8-10 To be forgiven for our sin, we must believe and confess that Jesus is Lord. Salvation comes through Jesus Christ.[1]

"All sin makes us sinners, and all sin cuts us off from our holy God. All sins, therefore, lead to death (because they disqualify us from living with God), regardless of how great or small they seem. Don't minimize 'little' sins or overrate 'big' sins. They all separate us from God, but they all can be forgiven." We cannot sin a sin that's too bad or too big for God to forgive.[2]

2. Record Romans 3:28.

Why does God save us by faith alone?
  Faith eliminates human pride.
  Faith exalts God, not people.
  Faith makes salvation available to all.
  Faith causes us to admit that we can't keep the law or measure up to God's standards—we need help.
  Faith is based on a relationship with God, not on performance for God.

From the Book of God's Revelation to John, we turn to the Gospel of John to discover truths we can use to encourage unbelievers to live a life in the Lord. We become new creatures. The Bible very specifically tells the believer who he or she is. You'll like what John has to say about you.

3. Record brief phrases in the Book of John that cause you to celebrate who you are in Christ:
  3:36   (Example) I have eternal life.
  5:24   (Example) I've passed from death to life.
  7:38
  8:32
  14:14
  14:20
  14:27
  15:9
  16:27
  17:9
  17:13
  17:15
  17:17
  17:18
  17:22
  17:23

4. What are the important truths that unbelievers must be told? There are five basic concepts that they must understand.
  (1) God offers eternal life to all who come to Him through His Son, Jesus. Summarize John 3:16 and John 10:10.

  (2) Sinful humanity has chosen to reject God's offer, choosing instead a way that leads to God's judgment and humanity's destruction. Record John 3:36.

  (3) God sent His Son to this world to pay the penalty for our sin and to take away our judgment by dying on a cross in our place. Record John 3:17.

  (4) To receive eternal life, we must repent of our sin, turn to Christ for forgiveness, and then surrender our entire life to Him. Read John 3:3 and John 6:47. Believing is more than simply acknowledging Christ in your mind. To believe is to permit Christ to have full control of every area of your life.

  (5) Eternal life can be yours for the asking. Pray something like this: *I confess that I am a sinner and that I need You. I believe that You paid the penalty for my sins when You died on the Cross so that I may have eternal life. Thank You, Jesus, for taking my punishment and providing forgiveness for me. I now invite You into my heart and surrender the control of my entire life to You. Help me to be what You want me to be. In Your name I pray. Amen.*

Now you are a believer, a Christian! Christ lives in you. He is all you need for living your new life. Learn to trust Him all the time, in all circumstances.

When you disobey the Lord, confess your sin immediately to Him and to those you have wronged. Talk to the Lord in prayer throughout your day. Read the Bible for spiritual food each day. Become involved with other believers. Find a church where God's Word is believed and taught. You need fellowship with your Christian brothers and sisters. Join others in studying God's Word and praying for each other.

Dear Lord, guide us to those who are longing to be believers but need someone to help and encourage them.

MEMORY CHALLENGE

What did God make known to the sons of Israel?

DAY FIVE

Silent Worship

Read Revelation 7:11-12.

1. Name the three groups standing around the throne.

2. What attitudes do you think are expressed by falling down before God?

3. What were they saying to God?

4. On a scale of 1 to 10 (with 1 being "terrible" and 10 being "terrific"), how would you rate the quality and consistency of your personal praise and worship life?

Worship continues to be a vital part in God's revelation to John. We must conclude from His revelation that worship will be an important role in heaven for everyone. How do we learn to worship? Can we enroll in "Worship 101"?

We can begin with the practice of inner prayer and worship. Our goal should be to pray and to worship the Lamb without ceasing.

Is it possible to practice continual communion with God? Is there a way of directing our thoughts on more than one level at a time? "One level we may be thinking, discussing, seeing, calculating—meeting all the demands of immediate circumstances. But deep within, behind the scenes, at a more profound level, we may also be in prayer and adoration, song and worship."[1]

The secular world of today values and cultivates only the first level of thinking. But in a godly culture, people know that the deep level of prayer and awareness of the Holy Spirit is the most important thing in the world. It's at this deep level that the real business of life is determined. In lowliness it knows joys, stabilities, peace, and assurances that are utterly unbelievable to the secular mind. The secular world cannot comprehend the blessings of a deep inner communion with Jesus.

Between the two levels is problem-solving interaction, but the emphasis must be upon the deeper level, at which the heart dwells in the presence and worship of the Lamb. The godly person brings all affairs of the first level down into the second level with the Light, holding them there in His presence and responding to them in spontaneous, incisive, and simple ways of obedience and faith. Much apparent wheat becomes worthless chaff, and some chaff becomes valuable wheat. As we practice submission to the Light within, we humbly begin to see all things through the eyes of God. In the second level, the life of God flows through the heart and soul of men in continual revelation and creative newness.

How do we grasp His life within and live a life of prayer and worship? By the quiet, persistent practice of turning to Him day and night in prayer and inward worship and surrender to Him who calls in the depth of our souls. Mental habits of an inward, secret turning to God must be established. After weeks and months and years of practice, and lapses and failures, we'll achieve habits of worship and prayer without ceasing.

Begin now, as you read these words, to offer your whole self in joyful abandon to Him who is within. With secret expressions of praise, turn in humble wonder and joy to Him. Keep in contact with the outer world. Walk and talk and work and laugh. But behind the activities of the day, keep up the life of simple prayer and inward worship. Keep it up throughout the day. Let inward prayer and worship be your last act before you fall asleep and your first act when you awake. In time you'll find, as Brother Lawrence described in *The Practice of the Presence of God* that "those who have the gale of the Holy Spirit go forward even in their sleep."[2]

The first days and weeks and months can be awkward and painful—but greatly rewarding. Awkward, because it takes constant vigilance and effort and recommitments of the will at the first level. Painful, because our lapses are so frequent, the intervals when we forget Him so long. Rewarding, because we've begun to live a deeper life.

Offer even your broken worship to Him. Accept no discouragement. Return quietly to Him, and find joy in His presence.

MEMORY CHALLENGE

Write out Psalm 103:7.

Atoning Blood

Read Revelation 7:13-17.

We are continuing to study one of the most beautiful scenes in Scripture. There is a large crowd of people, too numerous to count, from all nations, provinces, and languages standing in front of the throne and before the Lamb. They have on white clothing and are holding palm branches. With mighty shouts, they are praising God for salvation. All the angels are crowding around the throne and around the elders and the living creatures. They are falling facedown before the throne and worshiping God.

In verse 13 we read that one of the 24 elders asked John a question that sounds like one we would ask: "Who are they, and where have they come from?"

1. Did John know the answer?

2. Record the elder's answer in verse 14.

Many of us have tried several methods to remove the guilt of sin—good works, intellectual pursuits, and even blaming others. God was so patient with us, continuing to convict our sinful hearts. The time came when, by faith, we believed that salvation from sin's penalty can come only through Jesus Christ. Verse 14 gives us a word picture of how we are saved by faith. It is difficult to imagine how blood could whiten any cloth, but the blood of Jesus Christ is the world's greatest purifier—because it removes the stain of sin.

3. Record Isaiah 1:18.

Blood is the vital fluid circulating through the body. When the heart stops pumping blood through the body, there's no longer life in that body. Life is in the blood (Leviticus 17:11, 14); or the blood *is* the life (Deuteronomy 12:23). The blood represented the life, and so sacred is life before God that the blood of murdered Abel could be described as crying to God from the ground for vengeance (Genesis 4:10). Immediately after the Flood, the eating of the blood

of the animals was forbidden, although their slaughter for food was authorized (9:3-4; Acts 15:20, 29).

The loss of life is the penalty for sin, and its vicarious surrender (substitutional sacrifice) was necessary for remission of sin (Hebrews 9:22). So under the Mosaic law, the blood of animals was used in all offerings for sin. The blood of beasts killed while hunting or slaughtered for food was poured out and covered with dirt, because blood was withheld by God from people's consumption and reserved for purposes of atonement (Leviticus 17:1-14; Deuteronomy 12:15-16). "The blood of Jesus Christ" or "the blood of the Lamb" are figurative expressions for His atoning death.

4. According to Revelation 7:15, when do the people serve God?

5. What does God do for the people?

6. How does verse 16 describe their life in the shelter of God's tabernacle?

7. How will the Lamb be a shepherd to them?

In Revelation 7:1-8 we see believers receiving a seal to protect them through a time of great tribulation and suffering. In verses 9-17 we see the believers finally with God in heaven. All who have been faithful through the ages are singing before God's throne. Their tribulations and sorrows are over: no more tears for sins, for all sins are forgiven; no more tears for suffering, for all suffering is over; no more tears for death, for all believers have been resurrected to die no more!

Be there!

Written by Marie Coody

Recite Psalm 103:1-7 aloud.

Revelation

LESSON 8

■ A Study of Revelation 8

DAY ONE

Seventh Seal —Silence and Sorrows

Read Revelation 8, concentrating on verses 1-4.

1. When the seventh seal was broken, how long was the silence in heaven?

2. Why do you think there might have been this long silence? Write your own idea, then summarize the following scriptures for other ideas.

   Psalm 50:1-3, 21

   Isaiah 42:14-15

   Isaiah 57:11

   Daniel 4:19

   Habakkuk 2:20

3. To what did the angel who stood before the altar with the golden censer add the incense?

4. Did God ever withhold judgment for a time because of the prayer of His saints? Briefly summarize the two biblical stories below.

   2 Kings 19:14-19, 35-37

   2 Chronicles 20:6-17, 23-25

5. Could the prayers in Revelation 8:3 have been for justice? Read the parable of the persistent widow in Luke 18:1-8, recording verse 7 below.

6. God does as He wills in heaven and on earth, including bringing judgment and justice. Record 1 Samuel 12:16.

7. What went up before God out of the angel's hand (Revelation 8:4)?

MEMORY CHALLENGE

Psalm 103:8

The LORD is compassionate and gracious, slow to anger and abounding in lovingkindness.

8. Are the prayers of the saints sweet incense to God? Record Psalm 141:2.

The opening of Revelation 8 marks the opening of the seventh seal of the book that had been *in the right hand of Him who sat on the throne* (Revelation 5:1). The Lion of Judah, who had overcome, had taken and opened the book. Chapter 6 records the first six seals carried out by four horsemen and includes a false christ, war, famine, death, martyrs, and terror. As if this were not bad enough, the seventh seal ushers in the seven angels with seven trumpets, who open more judgments representing the beginning of sorrows.

When the Lion of Judah broke the seventh seal, there was an intermission of holy restraint known as silence. The pregnant pause indicated anticipation, mystery, awe, patient waiting, and expectation of the unknown. Was this like the six days that God had created and then rested, or was it the signaling of a catastrophe? Imagine a giant chess match in which the audience waits patiently, anticipating the next move. In his commentary on Revelation, Earl Palmer writes, "It communicates in a dramatic way the full and awesome authority of God. Everything must wait for his kingly move."[1] The silence makes the creatures sober regarding what's to come, and their response is prayer.

Prayer's importance was demonstrated after the silence. An angel (not one of the seven holding trumpets) held a golden censer that was filled with incense and added to the prayers of the saints. In the Old Testament, incense was a symbol of worship and prayers. The priests would burn a fragrant mixture upon the altar of incense, and the smoke would fill the Temple and ascend to heaven. Exodus 30:1-9 and 34-38 gives the details of the altar of incense and how Aaron and his priestly line were to burn the incense. *There shall be perpetual incense before the LORD throughout your generations* (verse 8). *The incense which you shall make . . . it shall be holy to you for the LORD* (verse 37). As the sweet fragrance of the incense goes up before the throne, so do the prayers of the saints. They are connected and intertwined. The praises of heaven cease so the prayers of the saints can be heard. Ray C. Stedman writes, "This silence comes as a dramatic contrast to the shouting of praise and the playing of harps that has been going on in heaven up to this point. Millions of angels, hosts of redeemed humans, and other heavenly creatures have been crying out before the throne of God and singing praises to Him. But now suddenly, everything ceases."[2] So the silence of heaven is caused by the prayers of the earthly saints.

Have you ever wondered if your prayers carry much weight? Daniel 9 relates the story of Daniel discovering the time of 70 years prophesied by Jeremiah for the desolation of Jerusalem. He realizes the time is at hand. As Daniel gave his attention to the Lord in prayer, God sent an angel—his prayer was heard! (Daniel 9:20-23).

God weighs the prayers of His people. Because of them, He postponed judgment for a time. And again, because of the prayers of His people, He proceeded to judge. How could that be?

The Lord is not slow about His promise, as some count slowness, but is patient toward you, not wishing for any to perish but for all to come to repentance (2 Peter 3:9). Our prayers for each other should be for forgiveness and grace, that all should come to salvation in Jesus Christ. But God ultimately wants to bring humanity to himself, and those who choose not to follow will have to be eliminated if there is to be peace and unity in God's kingdom. This is what God's judgment is all about. *Thy kingdom come. Thy will be done in earth, as it is in heaven* (Matthew 6:10, KJV). The time will come when grace is no longer available and judgment will prevail. This is demonstrated for us over and over in the Old Testament, where people or nations were given an opportunity to follow God. If they chose not to do so, they were wiped out. When Israel chose not to follow God, they lost wars, forfeited their promised land, and ended up in captivity. "To a world that rejects grace, God can bring peace only through judgment."[3]

During the time God withheld judgment, the saints prayed for salvation and grace for all people. But now the prayers change to prayers for judgment, for many have chosen to reject God's redemptive plan. Judgment is the only recourse, so in response to the prayers, God sets in motion the trumpet judgments. His judgment against His enemies will triumph, giving us, the Body of Christ, warning against complacency. The restraint of evil is lifted, and the earth plunges into chaos.

Revelation 8 will take us through the first four trumpet judgments, which are against the earth and are sometimes called "war trumpets." The latter three, called "woe trumpets," are against humanity, ending with Satan being cast out of heaven and producing a superman or beast. Certainly this is the beginning of sorrows, even greater than has already been seen on earth. The silence came before the storm.

May we be fervently at prayer for the salvation of all. May we seriously pray for an unsaved world, knowing that judgment will come if grace is not received.

DAY TWO

Seven Trumpets Sound

Read Revelation 8:5-6.

The angel throwing the fire from the altar to earth represents the prayers of the saints being cast upon the earth so that the judgments begin. The sounding a trumpet by angels marks each judgment.

1. Summarize the story of Jericho from Joshua 6:1-5, 15-16, and 20-21, emphasizing the use of seven angels and trumpets.

2. What was the purpose of the trumpets in the above story for *(a)* the children of Israel, and *(b)* the city of Jericho?

3. Four purposes are found for trumpets in Numbers 10:3-10. List them.

4. What else were trumpets used for in the Old Testament?

   Exodus 19:19. What was given in Exodus 20?

   Leviticus 23:24-25

   Leviticus 25:9 (Include what this day was.)

   1 Kings 1:34

   Joel 2:1

5. While John was given this revelation so the Church would know what would occur in the end times, he was also writing it in a letter to seven actual churches of his day. What could God have been trying to say to the churches through the trumpet judgments?

6. Does God sound a trumpet in our lives for any of the above reasons? Pick the ones you believe apply, and add other ideas of how He sounds a trumpet for you personally. Then record Proverbs 8:4.

The more we study our Old Testament, the more we understand Revelation. One theologian has said that all the signs and symbols of the last book of the Bible are found throughout God's Word. Studying the trumpets helps emphasize this.

But the trumpets of Revelation 8 are a call to judgment. The first four trumpet judgments seem particularly to relate to humanity's abuse of God's creation. When it comes to creation, it seems we go to extremes. One group, environmentalists, places a higher priority on creation than on people. The other group, represented by irresponsible big businesses and individuals, is so careless of God's creation that it is littered, polluted, or destroyed for profit.

Environmentalists spend an incredible amount of energy fighting for whales, walruses, and the spotted owl. Because we have not taken care of God's creation in the first place, these animals are threatened with extinction. This is not how God planned it, and we should consider trying to protect them. But when animals become more important than starving people, abused children, or refugees in dirty, rat-infested camps, we have lost sight of our priorities. God's Word tells us that He takes care of the sparrows, but the sparrow—or the spotted owl—does not have a soul. Human suffering due to poverty or sin deserves more of our attention than do animals.

An editorial by David A. Ridenour appeared in the *Daily Oklahoman* September 7, 1998. He reported that a potent chemical, toxol, comes from a tree known as the Pacific yew. Toxol holds great promise as a drug for some forms of ovarian, lung, and breast cancer. However, one of our major political figures is opposing this, because three trees are required to supply medicine for one patient. The point of Mr. Ridenour's article is "how little he cares about human suffering when his environmental values are at stake."[1]

I recently heard of a woman who was paying $10,000,000 to have her dog cloned. The dog was getting older, and she wanted one just like him when he died. Where are our priorities?

The other extreme is big businesses that, for the sake of money, dump poisonous chemicals into rivers, hazardous waste into landfills near water supplies, or those that cut down the rain forest at such amazing speed that the earth is in jeopardy of losing much of its oxygen supply. Individuals irresponsibly throw trash onto our highways, beaches, and mountainsides. Old-growth redwood trees are cut down because someone wanted a pretty veranda on their lake home. What's the balance? Must we go from one extreme to another?

The first four trumpets sound and tell us we will be judged for our abuse of the earth. Where do we fit in with this? Are we exercising balance in our approach? May each of us personally avoid judgment for God's creation by giving it care.

MEMORY CHALLENGE

Fill in the blanks:

The LORD is _____ and _____,

slow to _____ and _____ in

lovingkindness.

Psalm 103:8

After studying the harsh truth of today's lesson, remind yourself of God's goodness by reading the memory verse aloud three times. Praise Him for His mercy.

DAY THREE

Scorched

Read Revelation 8:7.

1. What happened when the first trumpet sounded?

2. Had this occurred on earth before? Look up these passages and describe the situation.

   Exodus 9:23-26

   Ezekiel 38:22

3. The purpose of the trumpet judgments in Revelation is to purify the earth of evil while humanity has a last chance for repentance. What was the purpose in the Old Testament? Zechariah 13:8-9 will help with your answer.

4. What do grass or trees represent in the following scriptures?

   Judges 9:7-15

   Psalm 92:7

   Daniel 4:20-22

5. Read Joel 1:1-7. This prophet first describes the literal plague of _____ and then switches to a prophetic invasion by enemy _____.

In the summer of 1988 a great fire raged in the famous Yellowstone National Park. Since national park policy is to let nature take its course, the blaze burned out of control for days. By the time the last flame flickered, 45 percent of Yellowstone had been affected in some way.

When the first angel sounds the trumpet, Revelation 8:7 tells us, a great fire will burn up all of the grass and one-third of the trees and earth. Is this event literal or symbolic?

Old Testament prophecy told us that Jesus Christ would be born in Bethlehem in Judah (Micah 5:2) of a virgin (Isaiah 7:14). When called to give His defense, He would be silent (53:7), and for His garments, lots would be cast (Psalm 22:18). This was literal. Prophecy also told us the Messiah would be a branch (Jeremiah 23:5), a cornerstone (Psalm 118:22), and a great light (Isaiah 9:2). The government would rest on His shoulders (verse 6), but God meant His government, not an earthly one. These prophecies were symbolic.

Were Jesus' miracles literal or symbolic? He literally fed the 5,000, but this is also symbolic of His power to supply all our earthly needs. Christ literally walked on water and even allowed Peter to join Him. This situation was also symbolic of His control over nature. Jesus called Lazarus from the dead after this friend of Jesus' had been in the tomb three days. The symbolism here was for His own resurrection after three days.

When we study Revelation, we should keep in mind that the words we read are both literal and symbolic. We know that at one point in the seven years of tribulation, hail and fire mixed with blood will rain down from the sky and scorch all the grass and one-third of the trees and earth. This will literally happen and put the earth in great distress. In the United States alone, we have only enough vegetation to provide our population with 60 percent of its needed oxygen. We depend on other parts of the earth, mainly the rain forest, to provide us with the other 40 percent. What happens to the oxygen supply when one-third of the earth's foliage is scorched?

Symbolically, grass in Scripture has always represented the common folk, while trees have represented kings or leaders and are often connected with independence and pride. Grass that is trampled under foot is symbolic of humanity's frailty and weakness.

So as we study the trumpet judgments, we know they have both literal and symbolic meanings. One-third of the earth's vegetation will be scorched, but this also tells us that leaders and the common humanity will be annihilated. Symbolically, humanity and the earth they were entrusted to care for will be judged and systematically destroyed. The only safeguard we have to keep us from being scorched is having Jesus Christ in our hearts as our Savior. May He find us faithful.

MEMORY CHALLENGE

How does Revelation 8:7 describe our Lord?

DAY FOUR

Ships and Seas

Read Revelation 8:8-9.

1. What happened when the angel sounded the second trumpet?

2. Had God ever done anything like this previously? Refer to Exodus 7:20-21.

3. Will God do anything like this again after the second trumpet? Summarize Revelation 16:3.

4. What does the sea represent in Scripture? (See Isaiah 57:20.)

5. Turn to Jeremiah 51:24-25 to record what mountains symbolize in the Bible.

6. What does Babylon symbolize in God's Word?

   Isaiah 47:1, 9-11

   Jeremiah 50:35, 38

7. How are those guilty of unbelief described in each of the following passages?

   Jeremiah 6:10

   Acts 7:51

   Ephesians 4:18

8. How are we to handle idolatry to avoid unbelief? Summarize these scriptures.

   1 Corinthians 10:14

   1 Thessalonians 1:9

1 John 5:21

None of us believed that a volcano in mainland United States that had been dormant since 1857 would erupt, spraying debris and ash 12 miles into the sky. But on May 18, 1980, Mount St. Helens in Washington state erupted violently, leveling thousands of acres of land with molten lava and killing great numbers of animals and birds in its path. Much of the mountain was blown away, sending ash far into surrounding states. The death total was believed to be 59.

In studying Mount St. Helens, we find that this volcano has erupted every 100 to 150 years for thousands of years. When St. Helens "blew her stack," it had been 123 years since the last eruption. Why were we surprised? According to its history, Mount St. Helens was right on time.

If God so chose, He could cause a volcano to erupt and throw itself into the ocean, creating death and destruction. Could He make it turn red? Read Exodus 7:2-21, which gives an account of the first plague against Egypt. The question is—why do we doubt that God is in control?

When Moses told the Egyptians that God would turn the water into blood, did they believe that was possible? No! In fact, they still did not believe in God's power by the time the 12th plague arrived, or they would have protected their firstborn.

The sea in this passage of Scripture represents a great nation or Babylon, which is the nation always referred to as evil in the Old Testament and Revelation. Their sin was unbelief as they chose to worship idols instead of the one true God. We are told to flee from idolatry because it promotes unbelief.

Remember: these are the trumpet judgments. Humanity's power compared to God's is like comparing the strength of an egg to that of a giant boulder. God will have His way—and right on time. Our work is to faithfully believe, avoiding idolatry, so that God can be our first priority.

"I am not afraid of storms, for I am learning how to sail my ship," wrote Louisa May Alcott.

MEMORY CHALLENGE

Summarize this week's memory challenge, using your own words.

DAY FIVE

Star of Wormwood

Read Revelation 8:10-11.

1. Describe what happens when the third angel sounds the trumpet.

2. Read the following scriptures. Describe what wormwood is.

   Deuteronomy 29:18

   Proverbs 5:4

   Jeremiah 9:15

3. What do we learn from God's Word regarding fallen stars? Summarize the following passages.

   Isaiah 14:12

   Matthew 24:29

4. Who could the star of wormwood be? Summarize the following scriptures.

   Ephesians 2:1-2

   Revelation 9:1

5. In this trumpet judgment, could the waters literally be bitter? Read Exodus 15:23-25 for an answer and short explanation.

6. What is the symbolic meaning of the waters? Refer to Revelation 17:15.

During the summer of 1998, Oklahoma and other Midwestern states in the United States experienced merciless heat and little rainfall. Without designed watering, grass, shrubs, and trees began to die. Problems like this are almost constant in much larger places like California. Then we move on to think of third world countries, where water systems have not been highly developed and people are constantly in need of clean water.

Now let's imagine a time when one-third of the world's water turns bitter and unusable. Is there any doubt we would be in trouble?

Wormwood is a bitter plant found in the Middle East. Its use in this passage relates to the destruction of one-third of the water supply. Symbolically, however, the star of wormwood is Satan himself. He is the star that fell from heaven, bringing all sorts of bitterness to the earth.

Ray C. Stedman in his sermon "Angels of Doom" imagines this star to be a comet that breaks up when it enters the earth's atmosphere and strews itself everywhere, including rivers, lakes, springs, and oceans. Whatever it touches would probably be poisoned. He questions whether perhaps God gave us a modern-day warning about this with the huge atomic accident in Russia at Chernobyl in 1986.[1] You see, "Chernobyl" in Russian means "wormwood."

When wormwood falls, it affects the water. But as Satan, it also affects people. Now let's imagine another interpretation of this that could be not only symbolic but also literal. What if this fallen star represents a highly visible Christian leader who suddenly denies Christ? Imagine this person being someone like Billy Graham or the pope. Can you fathom the repercussions? Many individuals with weak faith who look to these men for spiritual strength would be shaken and likely would fall. Christians everywhere would be wondering what in the world was happening.

The good news is that Satan is only a counterfeit, and Jesus is the Bright Morning Star. Second Peter 1:19 reads, *We have the prophetic word made more sure . . . until the day dawns and the morning star arises in your hearts.* We are promised that Morning Star in Revelation 2:28. Jesus speaks directly to us in Revelation 22:16, stating, *I am . . . the bright morning star.*

In the midst of much suffering, the Bright Morning Star brings us hope.

MEMORY CHALLENGE

Record Nehemiah 9:17.

DAY SIX

Smitten

Read Revelation 8:12-13.

1. What will happen when the angel sounds with the fourth trumpet judgment?

2. Describe the ninth plague on Egypt found in Exodus 10:21-23. What symbolism regarding light might you conclude from this passage?

3. Define the word "theophany," using a dictionary or Bible concordance.

4. Occasionally God chooses to reveal himself through forces of nature. Summarize the following scriptures, which show theophany for judgment through the use of light.

   Ezekiel 32:7-8

   Joel 2:10

   Matthew 27:35, 45

5. Record the following scriptures.

   John 9:5

   John 12:46

   2 Corinthians 4:6

6. If God removes physical light from the world, what does this mean He will also remove?

Light affects us emotionally and physically. Take a moment to consider what would happen if we had one-third less sunlight than we now have. Have you ever experienced a week of rain or overcast skies? A lack of sunshine might make us feel depressed. With less sunlight, could the same vegetation grow? What would happen to cities that depend on solar power?

Light also affects us mentally and spiritually. Why do people refuse to turn to God even after these trumpet judgments? Pharaoh and Egypt ignored the power of God through 12 plagues, even the plague of losing the firstborn son. They just would not accept the light. Modern humanity will be no different.

The first four trumpet judgments are to display God's power and might regarding humanity and earth. As each occurs, it gives people encouragement to repent and turn to God. The last three trumpets will become even more harsh, and it will be more difficult for people to repent. The fourth trumpet gives us in two ways a clue regarding this.

First, symbolically in the Bible the sun, moon, and stars are ruling authorities. As these are cut one-third, it means that the old order of government is broken up, making room for another. Enter the Antichrist to fill this gap. The world accepts him more easily because light has been dimmed, meaning restraint on earth is somewhat removed. There will be a great need for law and order, for someone to step in and be savior of the chaotic world. Satan's deceit is an evil carbon copy of God's plan. Remember that the devil parades *as an angel of light* (2 Corinthians 11:14).

Second, the Light of the World, Jesus, is being withdrawn from the earth. He warns us in John 12:35-36, *For a little while longer the Light is among you. Walk while you have the Light, so that darkness may not overtake you; he who walks in the darkness does not know where he goes. While you have the Light, believe in the Light, so that you may become sons of Light.* There will be a time the light is harder to walk in because the darkness will be great. Mentally and spiritually, we will not know what to do as when Christ's light shone in its fullness. Knowledge will decrease as people become more evil. Good judgment will go adrift as humanity no longer exercises *Your Word . . . a lamp to my feet and a light to my path* (Psalm 119:105).

We will lose much of the physical light of the sun. We will lose governmental authorities as symbolized by the sun, moon, and stars. But we will also lose the light of God's presence, meaning the restraint of evil will be lifted. All will be smitten as the eagle, a symbol of danger, flies

through the air to conclude Revelation 8. It is no wonder that the cry is *Woe, woe, woe to those who dwell on the earth* (verse 13). Our only hope is to *walk in the Light as He Himself is in the Light* (1 John 1:7).

Written by Linda Shaw

MEMORY CHALLENGE

Fill in the blanks from memory:

*Bless the L*ORD*, O my soul, and all that is _____ _____, bless His _____ _____. Bless the* L*ORD*, O my soul, and _____ none of His _____; who _____ all your _____; who heals all your _____; who redeems your _____from the pit, who crowns you with _____ and compassion; who satisfies your years with _____ _____, so that your _____ is renewed like the _____. The* L*ORD performs _____ deeds and _____for all who are oppressed. He made known His ways to _____, His acts to the sons of Israel. The* L*ORD is _____ and _____, slow to _____ and abounding in _____.*

Psalm 103:1-8

Revelation

■ A Study of Revelation 9

DAY ONE

Darkness

Read all of Revelation 9, concentrating on verses 1 and 2, and Ephesians 6:10-18.

1. The last three trumpets are called the "woe trumpets." Record the prediction of the eagle in Revelation 8:13.

2. What did John see when the fifth angel sounded the trumpet?

3. What was given to him, and what did he do with it?

4. The fifth trumpet signaled woes that go beyond use of the natural and are demonic in nature. Record the following scriptures.

   2 Peter 2:4

   Jude 1:6

In Revelation 11:7, the beast comes up out of the abyss, and in 20:1-3, Satan is bound and thrown into the abyss for a thousand years. Most Bible scholars believe the abyss to be only an intermediate place of punishment for fallen angels. The final place of punishment is the lake of fire and brimstone recorded in verses 10, 14-15.

5. It seems evident that the angels who fell from heaven with Satan (Revelation 12:7-9) are the two types of demons described in Scripture—those who are free and seeking to indwell people and lead them into defiance of God's will, and those who are confined in chains in the abyss, evidently because of some especially great sin. This "bottomless pit" is a horrible place; even the demons loose on earth are afraid of being sent there. Read Luke 8:30-31, and record verse 31.

John saw in his vision a star, fallen from heaven to earth, to whom was given the key to this bottomless pit. It seems apparent that the "star" is an intelligent being; the key was given to *him*, and *he* unlocked and opened the pit. It is not clear who this person is, and Bible scholars are not in agreement as to his identity. Some believe it to be Satan, who is described as having fallen from heaven (Isaiah 14:12-15; Luke 10:18; Revelation 12:7-9). Some believe it to have been Christ himself who holds the key of death and Hades (1:17-18; 3:7). Most commentators seem to believe it to be a good angel (20:1) to whom Christ has entrusted the key and given the authority to unlock the abyss and release the demons on an unrepentant world. Unlocking and opening the pit releases the smoke and creates the darkness seen by John. Sin and evil blot out spiritual light and bring darkness and affliction, disorder and confusion. Out of this smoke and darkness come forth the demonic creatures.

MEMORY CHALLENGE

Psalm 103:9

He will not always strive with us, nor will He keep His anger forever.

71

Despite these demons who will roam the earth and create all sorts of havoc and affliction, God will still be in control! Even the dwelling place of the enemies of God is not beyond God's power and control, and these freed inhabitants will still remain under His authority. The powers of evil are given a last chance to work on earth, a period of spiritual persecution unlike anything this world has ever seen. God will use the evil results to call unbelievers once again to repentance, even as He now uses the results of *our* sins to call *us* to repentance. Revelation 9:4 assures the believer that he or she will be spared from harm when this first woe is released at the sounding of the fifth trumpet.

6. According to Ephesians 6:12, what is our struggle against?

   What does Ephesians 6:13 tell us to do to successfully resist?

Do you know Jesus Christ as your Savior? Have you repented of your sins and accepted His loving forgiveness? Are you living in "radical obedience" to His will? If not, take time now and ask for forgiveness for your sins and accept Him as Lord of your life. *If we confess our sins, He is faithful and righteous to forgive us our sins and to cleanse us from all unrighteousness* (1 John 1:9). Jesus is the only defense against the powers of darkness. If you have accepted Christ and abide in Him, you are assured in God's Holy Word that you need not fear the demons nor the evil of any person on earth.

7. Summarize Romans 8:37-39.

   Record 1 John 4:4.

Because you have kept the word of My perseverance, I also will keep you from the hour of testing, that hour which is about to come upon the whole world, to test those who dwell on the earth (Revelation 3:10).

DAY TWO

Demons

Read Revelation 9:3-6 and Joel 1—2.

1. What came forth out of the smoke?

2. What were they told they were not to harm?

   Who were they told they were to hurt?

3. What were they forbidden to do?

   What were they permitted to do?

4. What will people seek and not find?

Out of the smoke arising from the opened pit, demonic creatures came forth in the form of locusts with the power to sting like scorpions. In his commentary on Revelation in *The Daily Study Bible Series,* William Barclay reports this collection of information on locusts by G. R. Driver in the *Cambridge Bible for Schools and Colleges:*

> The words of Joel and Revelation concerning locusts are not an exaggeration. Locusts breed in the desert and invade cultivated areas for food. They average about two inches long and have a four- to five-inch wingspan. They travel in columns 100 feet wide and as much as four miles long. A column of locusts can blot out the sun and reduce the visibility of even large objects to less than 200 feet.
>
> Locusts can cause unbelievable destruction. When they have finished and leave an area, every blade of grass is gone, trees are completely stripped of bark, no plant life is left, and the land looks as if it had been scorched by fire. Here is just one example of the damage they can cause: in 1866, a plague of locusts invaded Algiers and caused a famine so severe it resulted in the deaths of 200,000 people.

The head of a locust is shaped like a miniature horse's head, the noise of their wings is a roar similar to that of a tremendous waterfall, and the sound of their eating resembles that of the crackling of a prairie fire. When locusts are on the march, the sound resembles "a heavy rain falling on a distant forest" (Barclay), and nothing has ever been successful in stopping them. They just keep on coming in a steady column, climbing hills, descending into valleys, entering homes, and leaving behind an earth that is scorched and devastated.[1]

The eighth plague visited upon the Egyptians by the Lord when Moses was trying to lead the children of Israel out of the land of Goshen was a plague of locusts (Exodus 10:12-13). The invasion of locusts mentioned in Revelation 9 will be worse; those coming from the smoke of the pit are not common locusts. These are demonic and do not act like the locusts of the natural world. They are forbidden to attack vegetation; their attack is to be against *the men who do not have the seal of God on their foreheads* (Revelation 9:4).

These demonic locusts will have the same ability to sting as scorpions. The scorpion native to Palestine has a long tail, which curls upward and ends in a curved claw. It's from this claw that it stings and secretes its poison, a sting far worse than that of a hornet. It will occasionally cause death but usually is not fatal, causing severe pain lasting about two weeks. These demonic locusts will also be torturers, not destroyers; they will have power to inflict pain and torment that lasts for five months, but not to kill; their power will be limited. (The lifespan of a natural locust is about five months.)

For those who are victims of this locust plague, the intense pain and torment of mind and spirit will be so unbearable that they will long for death—but they will be unable to die. In the Old Testament, Job expressed his desire to die because of the anguish, pain, and torment Satan had brought upon him (Job 3:21-22; 7:15). *Beacon Bible Commentary* quotes two scholars' observations on this: "Cornelius Gallus, a Latin writer said, 'Worse than any wound is to wish to die and yet not be able to do so,' and Barclay *(The Revelation of John, The Daily Study Bible Series)* adds: 'Such will be the state of man that even death would be a relief and release.'"[2]

Those who escape this torment will be those with *the seal of God on their foreheads*, the faithful and true servants of God. If the rapture of the Church has already taken place, as many believe, this may refer to the 144,000 from the 12 tribes of Israel who have been saved, and their thousands of converts (Revelation 7:3-14). Their sealing would be related to their salvation (Ezekiel 9:4; 2 Corinthians 1:21-22; Ephesians 1:13). If the Church has not yet been raptured, this would include all believers. The world of demons has no power against God's people. *We know that no one who is born of God sins; but He who was born of God keeps him, and the evil one does not touch him* (1 John 5:18).

Do you know beyond any doubt that you are born of God and ready to go with Jesus Christ when His Church is taken from this world? Are you able to say with assurance that you have received God's free offer of salvation, that your sins have been forgiven and covered by the blood of Jesus? If so, you have the assurance that you will be spared from harm during this invasion of demonic locusts. Lift your heart and voice in praise and thanksgiving to the holy, almighty God!

MEMORY CHALLENGE

Who will not always strive with us, nor keep His anger forever?

DAY THREE

Devastation

Read Revelation 9:7-12 and Joel 1:4-6; 2:1-14, 25-26; 3:14-17.

John sees in his vision a plague of supernatural locusts. The Old Testament prophet Joel described a plague of locusts as a foreshadowing of God's coming judgment at the end times.

1. Find the verses in today's Scripture passages that refer to these descriptions of the locusts.

    Example:

Appearance	Joel __2:4__,	like horses _____
	Rev. _____,	_____
Faces	Rev. _____,	_____
Hair	Rev. _____,	_____
Teeth	Joel _____,	_____
	Rev. _____,	_____
Breastplates	Rev. _____,	_____
Sound of wings	Joel _____,	_____
	Rev. _____,	_____

2. Who is king over the locusts, and what are his names?

3. This woe is an incomplete judgment. There is still time for the unsaved to repent before final judgment and total destruction. God does not cause this suffering, but He permits it as another, stronger warning to lost humanity. In his commentary on Revelation, Tim LaHaye asserts that it would be an act of mercy on God's part to permit a person to be tormented for five months if that would bring him or her to Christ and spare the torment of a lost soul in hell for eternity.

    Record 2 Peter 3:9.

It will be a terrible time for sinful humanity when the worst of the demons, those now chained in the darkness of the pit, are loosened to work their evil, led by their king, the angel of the abyss. This king's name in Hebrew is Abaddon, which means "destruction," and in Greek is Apollyon, meaning "the Destroyer," and that will be the mission for him and his band of locust demons. This is not Satan; he and many of the evil spirits of his kingdom are free now to roam about and are constantly seeking to indwell and devour the human race (Ephesians 6:10-12; 1 Peter 5:8).

Missionaries serving in pagan lands tell of supernatural phenomena that can be accounted for only by an evil force. In countries with a strong Christian influence, the ability of demons to possess a person has been more limited because of the light shed by Christ and His followers—but as nations turn away from God and become more and more disobedient, evil increases. It is essential that Christians recognize this evil activity, stand firmly and publicly against it, and pray often for the leaders of the battle against these evils.

4. You may have experienced "locusts" in some area in your life. Many actively torment humanity. There are the "locusts" of addictions, which include such things as alcohol, harmful drugs, gambling, illicit sex, pornography, gossip, or dishonesty. Even positive things can become addictive if you allow them to control your life—work, television, or spending, for example. Some "locusts" create fear or anxiety in their victims. Have they destroyed your peace and joy?

    Read Joel 2:25-26, and summarize God's promise for restoration.

5. If we are truly sealed by God (Revelation 9:4) and have *put on the full armor of God* (Ephesians 6:11), we can rely on Him for strength and endurance to help us win the battle. The spiritual armor we must put on to resist evil is found in Ephesians 6:14-18. From these verses, list seven things that must be done to be victorious over the forces of evil.

    (1) Gird your loins with truth.

    (2)

    (3)

    (4)

    (5)

    (6)

    (7)

An extraordinarily talented man, a fairly new Christian, was victoriously and joyfully serving our church and his Lord and Savior. Gifted with an incredible musical ability, he blessed us and praised God with his many musical talents. His joy in Christ was contagious. As a result of painful experiences in his past, he had turned his back on God as a young man and had wasted his God-given talent in a life of sin. For some time, most of us were unaware that behind the cheerful countenance and enthusiastic testimony, the flashing smile and mischievous twinkle in his eye, he had experienced hurt and betrayal and now suffered pain and weakness from a disease that would eventually cause his premature death.

I was visiting with him as we waited for choir practice to begin when he told me how he regretted the wasted years of his life. He was thankful that God had granted him more time than his doctor had predicted and that he had been given the opportunity to serve Him with his talents and enjoy the love and fellowship he had found in our church.

In one of our Wisdom of the Word lessons, Jeannie had shared Joel 2:25-26 with us, along with her Spirit-inspired insights for its application for our lives. I shared Jeannie's teaching with him; he wanted to know where it was located. I looked it up in my concordance that night and wrote it out and gave it to him a few days later. He read it silently several times, and his eyes filled with tears. I asked if he had found this promise to be true in his life. His heartfelt reply left no doubt of his gratefulness for a loving God who had never given up on him, who had forgiven his sins, who had given him this time to serve Him, who had blessed his life with love and friendships. Yes, these blessings had made up for the years the "locusts" had eaten.

Have the "locusts" swarmed, crept, stripped, gnawed, and caused devastation in your life? Accept God's loving mercy and forgiveness, and allow Him to *make up to you for the years that the swarming locust has eaten. . . . You will . . . be satisfied and praise the name of the LORD your God, who has dealt wondrously with you* (Joel 2:25-26).

MEMORY CHALLENGE

What promise is found in Psalm 103:9?

DAY FOUR

Unbound

Read Revelation 9:13-16.

1. From what location did John hear a voice when the sixth angel sounded the trumpet?

2. What was the command given by the voice to the angel with the trumpet?

3. What has your study of Revelation taught you about the altar mentioned in verse 13? Use these verses to help you with your answer.

   Revelation 6:9-10

   Revelation 8:3-4

This is the heavenly altar upon which the Israelites patterned the altar of incense in their tabernacles and in the Temple at the direction and command of God (Exodus 30:1-10). The altar of incense stood before the holy place, and incense was burned before the first and after the last sacrifice of the day. The prayers of the saints in Revelation represent a fragrant sacrifice to God.

4. Record Psalm 141:2.

5. For what reason were the four bound angels released?

6. How many horsemen did John see in his vision, and how did he know the number of them?

The first woe is past (Revelation 9:12); the second woe has come.

When the sixth trumpet sounds, John hears *a voice from the four horns of the golden altar which is before God* (verse 13). The voice commands the angel with the trumpet to release four angels who are bound at the river Euphrates. These four angels are not God's holy angels, or they would not have been bound. It seems most likely they were evil angels who were so eager to wreak havoc on humanity that God had to restrain and bind them until *the hour and day and month and year* (verse 15), the exact time He had prepared for their release. The locusts of the first woe had not been killers; they had been tormentors and torturers. These angels, and their host of followers, are killers. Releasing them brings about a floodtide of destruction on earth; one-third of the remainder of humanity are to be killed.

7. Record the words of Jesus in Matthew 24:21-22.

The Euphrates River is prominent in Scripture and has had a great deal of significance in the history of the world. It was one of four rivers that flowed out of the Garden of Eden (Genesis 2:10-14), where Adam committed the first sin (3:1-6). The first murder (4:8) no doubt took place somewhere not far from the Euphrates. It marked the eastern boundary of the land God promised Abraham and his descendants (15:18; Joshua 1:4). The Euphrates has traditionally been considered the boundary between the East and the West and marks the present division between the Near East and the Far East. A majority of the earth's population lives beyond the Euphrates.

The four angels, prepared to kill one-third of humanity, are able to raise vast armies immediately to carry out their mission. John sees armies of 200 million horsemen. All of the combined armies, Allied and Axis, during World War II numbered only about 70 million. Some Bible scholars think the tremendous number of 200 million is simply symbolic of the fact that there are far too many to count. However, John reports that he *heard the number of them* (Revelation 9:16).

The Bible tells us that sometimes God's plans and purposes are beyond our ability to fully grasp or understand. Some of the details of Revelation 9 are not absolutely clear, and the best of Bible scholars are not always in full agreement as to their meaning. However, as Josh McDowell and Don Stewart remind us in their book *Answers to Tough Questions*, "We do know that God is all-wise and all-knowing and that He has reasons for allowing things to happen that are beyond our comprehension."[1]

8. Record these verses.

Isaiah 55:8-9

Romans 11:33

If you know Christ Jesus as your Savior and are living in obedience to God's will for your life, you can trust His promise of eternal life (John 5:24; Titus 1:2). There may be persecution or even death, but if you remain faithful to the end, as God's child you can be secure in the knowledge that *I know whom I have believed and I am convinced that He is able to guard what I have entrusted to Him until that day* (2 Timothy 1:12).

Dear Lord, guide us to those who are longing to be believers but need someone to help and encourage them.

MEMORY CHALLENGE

What warning is found in Psalm 103:9?

Unmerciful

Read Revelation 9:17-19.

1. Describe the breastplates of the riders on the horses.

2. *The horses' heads are like the _____ _____ _____; their tails are like _____ and have _____.*

3. *Out of their mouths proceed _____ and _____ and _____.*

4. Where is the power of these horses located?

John sees in his vision 200 million horses and their riders. The breastplates of the riders were fiery red, the color of fire; hyacinth (jacinth), which is a dark, smoky blue, like the color of smoke rising from a large fire; and a sulfurous yellow, the color of brimstone. The horses' heads were like the heads of lions, and their power was in their mouths and tails. Their tails were like serpents and had heads and could inflict harm. Apparently it is the horses, and not their riders, who kill and destroy. Out of the mouths of the horses came fire, smoke, and brimstone. These three "plagues" killed one-third of humanity. The "plagues" of fire, smoke, and brimstone could be manifested in immediate death caused by the horrific breath of the horses or could be manifested in pestilence and epidemics of disease. (Some students of prophecy equate this demon invasion with instruments of modern warfare, suggesting that John's description could be of gunpowder and tanks, with which he would not have been familiar.)

This is not a natural phenomenon, but a literal description by John of unnatural evil spirits. Even those evil angels would not have been able to marshal such vast armies of men so quickly; this must be an invasion by the demon world. These evil spirits are utterly cruel and unmerciful. However, even these strange, warlike creatures are limited in their power. They are permitted to kill only one-third of remaining humanity; their days are to be cut short *for the sake of the elect* (Matthew 24:22). One-fourth of humanity have already been killed by the fourth horseman of the Apocalypse, whose name was Death, as a result of the sword, famine, pestilence, and wild beasts (Revelation 6:8). Over one-half of the population of earth have now

died, and one-third of the earth and trees and all the grass has been burned up, one-third of the sea had become blood, killing one-third of the sea life and destroying one-third of the ships. One-third of the fresh water is bitter and undrinkable, and one-third of the light of the sun, moon, and stars is gone. You would expect that this devastation would get the people's attention and bring about repentance. In his commentary on Revelation, J. Vernon McGee reminds us that "the problem with men who come to Revelation and say that it is difficult to understand and impossible to interpret is that they do not believe it. If you simply believe it and read it, it is very clear. Hellish forces will be at work during this period."[1]

5. This is still not a final and complete judgment. There will still be time for the remaining ungodly to repent and turn to God. You have recorded 2 Peter 3:9 in previous lessons; write out this verse once again.

   Record 1 Thessalonians 5:9.

6. Have you obtained salvation through our Lord Jesus Christ?

For God so loved the world, that He gave His only begotten Son, that whoever believes in Him shall not perish, but have eternal life (John 3:16). *God has given us eternal life, and this life is in His Son. He who has the Son has the life; he who does not have the Son of God does not have the life* (1 John 5:11-12). *If we confess our sins, He is faithful and righteous to forgive us our sins and to cleanse us from all unrighteousness* (1:9).

7. According to 1 Thessalonians 5:11, what should Christians be doing for one another?

Now may the Lord of peace Himself continually grant you peace in every circumstance. The Lord be with you all! (2 Thessalonians 3:16).

MEMORY CHALLENGE

Fill in the blanks:

He will not _____ _____ with us,

nor will He _____ _____ _____

forever.

Psalm 103:9

Unrepentant

Read Revelation 9:20-21; Psalm 51:1-17.

1. One-third of remaining humanity are killed during the second woe. Do those still living repent and turn to God?

2. List the five sins of the ungodly that John names here.

Read Romans 1:18-32.

3. What is the wrath of God revealed against (verse 18)?

4. What has been clearly seen, and how is it understood (verse 20)?

5. For what did they exchange the glory of God (verse 23)?

6. *They exchanged the _____ of God for a _____, and _____ and _____ the creature [created things, NIV] rather than the _____, who is blessed forever (verse 25).*

7. Do the ungodly know that the penalty for sin is death, and does this change their behavior (verse 32)?

Humanity fails to repent. They harden their hearts and stubbornly persist in rebellion against God. They continue to worship idols and demons. Biblical writers believe that their worship of idols is really demon worship, and their evil deeds and immorality are a result. Idolatry and immorality have always gone hand in hand. This pagan worship of idols that cannot see, nor hear, nor walk has created a people who do not have eyes to see Jesus, nor ears to hear the Word of God (Matthew 13:15). When God's works and His words are continually ignored and rejected, our hearts become hardened (Jeremiah 17:23), and we will reap the judgment (Ephesians 5:5-6; Hebrews 10:26-31).

8. Record Proverbs 29:1.

9. Read Isaiah 13:6-16, and summarize verse 9.

The results of idol and demon worship are murder, immorality, and thievery, and all have been forbidden in the Ten Commandments (Exodus 20:1-18). Sorcery is another product of idolatry. The word "sorcery" comes from the same Greek word as for "pharmacy" and can also indicate widespread use of drugs for evil purposes. We are already witnessing an increase in alcoholism and drug addiction, especially in our youth. Lust, promiscuity, fornication, adultery, and unnatural sex (Romans 1:26-27) are pervasive in our society. We are being prepared for the complete moral breakdown John foretells in Revelation 9:20-21. John sees a totally unrepentant people in his vision; those persons not killed in the first six trumpets apparently learned nothing, but, as Pharaoh did, they hardened their hearts and continued to disobey and reject God (Exodus 7:13, 22; 8:15, 32; 9:34-35; and others).

Those who indulge in sin will not inherit the kingdom of God (1 Corinthians 6:9-10). But our rebellion and rejection grieve the heart of God (Genesis 6:5-6). Thankfully, He has provided salvation and an inheritance in His kingdom for those who repent and accept Christ as Savior.

Come, let us worship and bow down, let us kneel before the LORD our Maker. For He is our God, and we are the people of His pasture and the sheep of His hand. Today, if you would hear His voice, do not harden your hearts (Psalm 95:6-8).

Repent, for the kingdom of heaven is at hand (Matthew 3:2; 4:17).

[If] you will seek the LORD your God . . . you will find Him if you search for Him with all your heart and all your soul. When you are in distress and all these things have come upon you, in the latter days you will return to the LORD your God and listen to His voice. For the LORD your God is a compassionate God; He will not fail you nor destroy you (Deuteronomy 4:29-31).

If you have not accepted God's loving invitation to repent of your sins and serve Him in obedience, He is giving you another opportunity right now. Read Psalm 51:1-17 and sincerely pray this prayer of David for pardon, and God will graciously forgive you. When David prayed this beautiful prayer for forgiveness, he had committed covetousness, adultery, stealing, and murder. No sin is too great for God to forgive when we truly repent. Come to God just as you are.

Written by Helen Silvey

MEMORY CHALLENGE

Quote Psalm 103:9 from memory. See if you can quote Psalm 103:1-9 with your small group.

Revelation

LESSON 10

■ A Study of Revelation 10

Presence of God

Read Revelation 10, concentrating on verses 1-2.

Revelation 10 begins with an interlude between the sixth and seventh trumpets. This is similar to the pregnant pause between the sixth and seventh seal (Revelation 8:1), when there was silence in heaven for half an hour. Revelation 5 is also interpreted as an intermission to the narrative. Chronologically the story is not advanced, but information is added to what has already been prophesied. The seventh trumpet judgment is not revealed until Revelation 11:15.

This is not the first time a strong or mighty angel has appeared. In Revelation 5:2, a strong angel held the book with the seven seals. Not every commentator agrees that these angels are one and the same. They do agree that this angel is not one of the seven trumpet angels. This strong angel has a different role, which we will see as we study Revelation 10.

1. Describe the angel mentioned in verse 1.

2. What are clouds symbolic of in Scripture? Give ideas from the following passages.

   Exodus 16:10

   1 Kings 8:10-12

   2 Chronicles 5:13-14

3. The rainbow in Scripture represents God's _____ with humanity (Genesis 9:16-17) and the _____ of God's divine glory (Ezekiel 1:28).

4. Read Exodus 34:29 and Matthew 17:2. Why did Moses' and Jesus' faces shine?

5. How would you define the presence of God? You may use some aids to research this if necessary.

6. What can we expect in the presence of God? Use Psalm 16:11 for your answer.

Psalm 103:10

He has not dealt with us according to our sins, nor rewarded us according to our iniquities.

7. How do you personally experience God's presence? If you have never experienced His presence, what is the first step you need to take to correct this?

In the United States we have two unique expressions that relate to the strong angel. First, we may say that someone has his or her "head in the clouds." By that, we mean that the person is idealistic, always dreaming, or not in touch with what's really going on. The other expression is that one has "both feet on the ground." Such a person is realistic and has good, common sense. He or she thinks things through, weighs the facts, and therefore makes sound judgments.

When we experience God's presence, both of these expressions could describe us. We are aware of the mystical part of God that, by earthly standards, puts our "heads in the clouds." But we are also firmly entrenched in the reality that God is in control of our lives and world. We may be thinking of our Heavenly Father and heavenly things. Our minds might be absorbed with prayer, His beauty in a daffodil, or even working through a spiritual lesson. Yet we also must have wisdom and knowledge about life that is practical and mundane that helps us exercise good judgment. We recognize that we have to live in the flesh and practice how to do this well.

To live in God's presence, we must have this balance of spirituality and reality. The angel obviously came from the very presence of God because of the meaning and symbolism of his attire. Yet he came to earth to John, a man still living bound to the earth. John was experiencing God's presence, yet while he was being given a vision of things to come, he was also able to deliver it to his fellow human beings, a very earthly job.

The strong angel was sent to do a job, but he was also sent to represent the presence of God. May we, too, keep our "heads in the clouds" of God's presence while we keep "both feet on the ground" as we live out His plan for our lives.

DAY TWO

Power of God

Read Revelation 10:2-4.

1. Where did the strong angel place each foot to stand?

2. How did the mighty angel cry out, and what happened after he did?

3. Read Psalm 29. What are the seven "thunders" of God's voice in verses 3-9?

4. List ideas from the following scriptures regarding God's power over nature.

   Genesis 1:1

   Psalm 78:26

   Psalm 93:1

   Jeremiah 51:15-16

5. List three of Jesus Christ's miracles that you would consider to be God's power over nature.

6. Deuteronomy 11 describes the rewards of obedience. Summarize verse 24 to capture what God promised the children of Israel if they obeyed.

The land and sea represent the sum total of the earth. There are no other parts than these two. In Scripture, the land and sea represent size and power. God's power is evident in the symbolism of Revelation 10:2-4. The power of God's voice is apparent as it thunders when the angel calls out in a loud voice. This passage also emphasizes the authority of heaven over earth.

In Revelation 10, the land and sea are mentioned three times. That tells us something of its importance. The sea is always mentioned first. Usually we mention land first. But the point of the strong angel standing with one foot on the land and one on the sea is that with God it makes no difference. He has an equal amount of power on land or water.

When I was growing up, my family liked to fish for cutthroat trout on Yellowstone Lake in Yellowstone National Park. Even though it was a 22-hour drive from our home, we went every summer for about 10 years. Back then, we could troll without any bait, and everyone in a large party could catch his or her limit in a day.

But Yellowstone Lake was known for its sudden storms. A beautifully clear blue sky could turn dark and ominous in five minutes. High winds could kick up, and the rain could pour forth from the heavens, putting fishermen in instant danger. The National Park Service had strict limits about how far one could go from shore due to this twist of nature.

One summer some of my family and friends were trolling for trout in our army raft when just such a situation came up. I remember my dad requiring us to get down on the floor of the raft while he set the trolling motor on full power and headed for shore. The waves got high, threatening to swamp the boat, coming over the edges and soaking us with cold, cold water. The rain came down like a showerhead turned to full blast. My memory can taste the fear I had of not making it back to shore before the raft was overturned. I'm sure I wasn't the only one praying!

When the disciples had a similar experience, Jesus walked to them on the water. His first words were, *Take courage; it is I, do not be afraid* (Mark 6:50). You see, it did not matter if Jesus was walking on land or sea. It was all surefootedness to Him. He could make any surface as solid as He wanted. Christ has the power of God.

This passage about the mighty angel on land and sea is a passage about God's power. There is none like Him. When He speaks, it is with power and authority, for He has all control over the entire universe.

MEMORY CHALLENGE

How does Ezra 9:13 relate to this week's memory scripture?

DAY THREE

Promise—No More Delay!

Read Revelation 10:5-6.

1. By whom did the mighty angel swear?

2. What was the description of God used in these verses?

3. Read Revelation 6:10. What was the question of the ones who had been slain?

4. God promises us there will be judgment for the evil when their time is come. Summarize the following verses.

   Numbers 16:25-26, 31-33

   Psalm 75:2-3

   Isaiah 47:10-11

   Joel 2:1-3

5. In Revelation 10:5-6, God is promising His people there will no longer be any delay for _____.

6. Explain why this is a good thing.

The Book of Proverbs repeatedly contrasts the righteous person with the evil person. Words used to describe the righteous in this book include "wise," "godly," "good," "blameless," and "upright." Words that describe the evil include "wicked," "foolish," "worthless," "treacherous," and "adulterous." Keeping this in mind, read some of the promises for the righteous and evil.

Proverbs 1:24-26: *Because I called and you refused, I stretched out my hand and no one paid attention; and you neglected all my counsel and did not want my reproof; I will even laugh at your calamity; I will mock when your dread comes.*

Proverbs 1:28-31: *Then they will call on me, but I will not answer; they will seek me diligently but they will not find me, because they hated knowledge and did not choose the fear of the LORD. They would not accept my counsel, they spurned all my reproof. So they shall eat of the fruit of their own way and be satiated with their own devices.*

Proverbs 1:33: *He who listens to me shall live securely and will be at ease from the dread of evil.*

Proverbs 2:7-8: *He stores up sound wisdom for the upright; He is a shield to those who walk in integrity, guarding the paths of justice, and He preserves the way of His godly ones.*

Proverbs 2:20-22: *So you will walk in the way of good men and keep to the paths of the righteous. For the upright will live in the land and the blameless will remain in it; but the wicked will be cut off from the land and the treacherous will be uprooted from it.*

Proverbs 3:13, 16-18: *How blessed is the man who finds wisdom. . . . Long life is in her [wisdom's] right hand; in her left hand are riches and honor. Her ways are pleasant ways and all her paths are peace. She is a tree of life to those who take hold of her, and happy are all who hold her fast.*

Proverbs 3:33: *The curse of the LORD is on the house of the wicked, but He blesses the dwelling of the righteous.*

Proverbs 4:18-19: *The path of the righteous is like the light of dawn, that shines brighter and brighter until the full day. The way of the wicked is like darkness; they do not know over what they stumble.*

Proverbs 6:12-15: *A worthless person, a wicked man, is the one who walks with a perverse mouth, who winks with his eyes, who signals with his feet, who points with his fingers; who with perversity in his heart continually devises evil, who spreads strife. Therefore his calamity will come suddenly; instantly he will be broken and there will be no healing.*

Proverbs 7:24-27: *Now therefore, my sons, listen to me, and pay attention to the words of my mouth. Do not let your heart turn aside to her [adulteress] ways, do not stray into her paths. For many are the victims she has cast down, and numerous are all her slain. Her house is the way to Sheol, descending to the chambers of death.*

Proverbs 8:35: *He who finds me [wisdom] finds life and obtains favor from the* LORD.

Certainly for the righteous there are promises of good things, while the evil can count on eventual judgment and eternal death. Yet when we live in the midst of evil, it sometimes becomes wearisome to put up with it. We begin wondering, "Will these people ever be punished for their evil?" The answer is yes. One day God will say, "Enough! I will delay no longer. The time is now." Then righteous judgment will come, and the spell of evil will be broken. Once again, the world will be pure as God intended it. God has said it, and we can count on it.

MEMORY CHALLENGE

Does God deal with us according to our sins or reward us according to our iniquities?

Is this also true of the evil person we studied about today, or only for the righteous?

DAY FOUR

Perplexities

Read Revelation 10:7.

1. What is going to be finished when the seventh angel sounds his trumpet?

2. In your opinion, to what might *the mystery of God* refer?

3. Summarize the following scriptures that speak of *the mystery of God.*

   Deuteronomy 29:29

   Romans 16:25

   Colossians 2:2

   1 Timothy 3:9

4. Is the angel telling John that secrets of prophecies in the past are now to be revealed? Look up Daniel 8:26 and 12:9 to help with your answer.

5. Read Luke 8:9-10. Jesus said His disciples would understand His words while others would hear only parables. Discuss the possibility that we as His disciples can understand the Book of Revelation to some degree while to others it is just perplexity.

6. When there is no more delay, what will happen to *the mystery of God?* Summarize Jeremiah 31:34.

When the Bible refers to *the mystery of God*, it often means the whole context of the gospel as far as the atoning death and exaltation of Christ. But another perplexity of God is His overall plan. Why would He allow Satan to reign for a period of time? Why give him that kind of power? What needs to happen for this to be satisfied before God will overpower Satan? God has ruled and overruled on earth, but He has never reigned. This will happen only when He strips Satan of all power for all time. It will happen only when the Book of Revelation is acted out completely.

Daniel Defoe wrote a well-known book by the name of *Robinson Crusoe*. In this book, Robinson Crusoe was stranded on an island of cannibals. One of these savages by the name of Friday became his companion. Robinson taught him the English language and basic knowledge of God. One day Robinson was explaining the power of the devil to Friday when Friday posed this question, "Well, but you say God is so strong, so great, is He not much strong, much might as the devil?" When Robinson answered, "Yes," Friday continued, "God is much stronger than the devil, but if God much strong, much might as the devil, why God not kill the devil?" Robinson was stumped! Instead of answering, he sent Friday to another part of the island to run an errand, hoping he would forget the question.

Can finite humanity understand God? Are we going to comprehend what everything means? Absolutely not! There are some perplexities we won't understand until we're on the other side, in heaven, with God. Look back over your life. Has God allowed some things to happen that you don't understand? Sometimes we just have to say, "I'm going to set that situation on the shelf and leave it there until I see Jesus face-to-face. Then it will all be revealed." It's a matter of faith. We don't know why or what it means, but we trust in God.

MEMORY CHALLENGE

Fill in the blanks:

He has not _____ with us according to our

_____, nor _____ us according to our

_____.

Psalm 103:10

DAY FIVE

Pleasingly Sweet, Yet Bitter

Read Revelation 10:8-10.

1. How many times in these verses was John told to take the book?

2. What did the angel tell John would happen after he took the book and ate it?

3. Read the parable of the sower and its explanation in Matthew 13:3-8, 18-23. How was God's Word both sweet and bitter to the seed that fell on rocky places?

4. There is much symbolism in God's Word of how our walk with Him is both bitter and sweet. Fill in the chart below by reading the scripture and telling what is bitter and what is sweet.

Sweet	*Bitter*
Psalm 119:103 (Example: *the Word*)	Psalm 32:5
Malachi 3:1	Ezekiel 3:1, 17-18
John 8:32	Romans 7:19
1 Kings 8:56	Ezekiel 2:8-10

5. Personalize the following scriptures by putting your name in them.

   Psalm 34:8

   Jeremiah 15:16

According to William Barclay, when Jewish boys were schooled to learn their alphabet, the letters were written on a slate with a mixture of honey and flour. Each boy was taught the letters, and then as he learned them and could say them correctly, he was rewarded with getting to eat the mixture.[1] Maybe John's vision was a throwback to this custom he had possibly experienced.

So often little joys are not just given to us; we must work for them. It is interesting that John was not given the little book to eat, but twice he was told to take it. Then he had to eat it. Something was required of John in his revelation. Something is required of us also in our walk with God.

We can admire how food looks on our plate, push it around with a fork, and even taste it—yet later spit it out. The same is true of God's Word. If we really want to know God, we must take His Word, put it into our mouths, chew it up, swallow it, and digest it. That is the only way He is truly going to become ours.

His Word is sweet, but as it reveals our sin, it becomes bitter. It may be sweet to be the messenger of God, but when the message is one of judgment, it may be bitter to deliver. It is so sweet to accept His Word, yet to try and live it day by day can indeed be bitter. Sweet are His promises, but in trusting them and waiting for them, there can be suffering and sorrow.

Isn't sweetness and bitterness true of all of life? Going shopping to buy a new wardrobe is so sweet until we get the bitterness of the bill. Finding a new romance is sweetness until it goes sour. Learning of the pregnancy of a much-wanted child is sweet until the bitterness of a miscarriage. Life is sweet and bitter. Why would it be any different in our walk with God?

John's revelation was so exhilarating, joyful, and mysterious—sweet. But it was a revelation of judgment bringing much suffering and sorrow. How bitter to have to write about that to the seven churches!

We, too, are invited to share in Christ's sweetness and bitterness. *While they were eating, Jesus took some bread, and after a blessing, He broke it and gave it to the disciples, and said, "Take, eat; this is My body." And when He had taken a cup and given thanks, He gave it to them, saying, "Drink from it, all of you; for this is My blood of the covenant, which is poured out for many for forgiveness of sins"* (Matthew 26:26-28). We cannot take God the Father and His Son, Jesus Christ, without eating of Him. Sometimes that will be sweet, and sometimes it will be bitter. But always, in the long run, it will be blessed.

MEMORY CHALLENGE

Recite the promise of Psalm 103:10 aloud.

DAY SIX

Prophecy

Read Revelation 10:11.

1. What was John told to do at the conclusion of this chapter?

2. Was anyone else ever given the same instruction? Summarize the following scriptures to answer the question.

    Jeremiah 1:9-10

    Ezekiel 3:1-4

3. Write the definitions of "prophecy" and "prophesy," using a dictionary or Bible concordance.

4. What was John's prophecy concerning? Would this include us?

5. How does this prophecy affect us today?

6. Was God's prophecy ever ignored in the past? As a challenge, find one Scripture reference to answer this. Summarize the passage you find.

John was attentive to the Word of God and obedient to the will of God. When he was told to take the book and eat it, he did so. Then he was told to tell through his letter to the seven churches—and consequently to the entire world eventually—what was to come. John is to warn the people again. This is the purpose of the Book of Revelation, and it is reiterated often. We are to hear from John the same message Ezekiel delivered. Death results when the righteous person turns to evil, and life results when the righteous person heeds the warning of prophecy and does not sin (Ezekiel 3:20-21).

Both Ezekiel and John ate a little book or scroll before they delivered their message. As we learned in yesterday's lesson, this indicates genuinely taking the message in before delivering it. "By the symbolism of the eating of the scroll, he indicates the necessity of assimilating his message, of making his message a part of himself, as a prerequisite to its delivery."[1] Certainly a prophet would need to really believe in his message in order to deliver it. A teacher or preacher of God's Word must do the same to be effective. Glaphre' Gilliland, founder of PrayerLife, believes one should never teach something that has not been perfected in his or her own life.

So John is to hear the message, believe it, and then deliver it to the whole world, including us. The purpose of this is to warn us of the importance of righteousness. It gives us opportunity to turn from our sin and be cleansed by the blood of the Lamb. That is why this message is still relevant today. These events have not yet happened, so we still have time to repent and become the children of God.

The end of Revelation 10 is also important because another big event is about to occur. The Antichrist is about to burst onto the scene. It's important to recognize that all the events in chapters 1—10 of Revelation must take place before the arrival of the Antichrist. Second Thessalonians 2:3-4 says, *Let no one in any way deceive you, for it will not come unless the apostasy comes first, and the man of lawlessness is revealed, the son of destruction, who opposes and exalts himself above every so-called god or object of worship, so that he takes his seat in the temple of God, displaying himself as being God.* While chapter 10 of Revelation starts with the mighty angel and ends with John's prophecy, we now move forward to the two witnesses (prophets) in chapter 11 and then the Antichrist, who will come later. Don't go away—there's more prophecy to come!

Written by Linda Shaw

MEMORY CHALLENGE

As much as possible from memory, write out Psalm 103:1-10.

Revelation

LESSON 11

■ A Study of Revelation 11

DAY ONE

The Holy City

Read all of Revelation 11, noticing the references to the Holy City in verses 2, 8, and 13.

1. What is the Holy City? Refer to Isaiah 52:1 if needed for this answer.

2. All the events of Revelation 11:1-14 take place in Jerusalem. Briefly summarize these events.

3. What other important events in the Bible took place in Jerusalem? List the events with the scriptures below.

   2 Samuel 5:6-7

   2 Samuel 6:12

   Nehemiah 12:27

   Matthew 21:8-10

   Matthew 23:37

   Acts 1:12; 2:1-4

   Acts 21:30-32

4. Place a star beside the above events that are evil.

5. In Revelation 11:8, Jerusalem is compared to Sodom and Egypt. What do each of these places represent? Summarize the following scriptures.

   Genesis 13:13

   Exodus 18:10

The Holy City, "el-Kuds" in Arabic, is part of the ancient history of the world while always playing an important role with the Hebrew people. It first appears in the Bible in Genesis 14:18 when the king of Salem, Melchizedek, brought out bread and wine to Abraham after he saved his nephew, Lot, who had been carried off with the men of Sodom in war. Salem later became Jerusalem.

When the Israelites entered Canaan, Jerusalem was ruled by a Semite king and occupied by Amorites and Jebusites. Joshua defeated its king but never entered the city. It was on the border of the assigned territory of two tribes, Benjamin and Judah, but occupied by foreigners. This was a reproach to the Promised Land, for the Israelites were to drive out all foreigners. David gained possession during one of his earliest campaigns as king, even though the inhabi-

---

MEMORY CHALLENGE

Psalm 103:11

*For as high as the heavens
are above the earth,
so great is His lovingkindness
toward those who fear Him.*

tants believed their city to be impregnable (2 Samuel 5:6-9). He then made it the capital of Israel, and Jerusalem became known also as "the City of David." He brought the ark of the covenant there to dwell in a tent. Later, his son Solomon built the Temple in Jerusalem as a place of worship, to house the ark and to be a place for God's presence to dwell.

In 586 B.C. Nebuchadnezzar captured the city and carried off most of its population, leaving only the very poorest people. He burned the Temple and palaces and broke down the city's walls. The city laid in waste for 70 years until the events of Ezra and Nehemiah began to take place to restore the city, wall, Temple, and population.

The Holy City was then ruled, in order, by the Persians, Greeks, Egyptians, Maccabees, and, at the time of Christ, the Romans. Herod the Great repaired the walls, rebuilt the Temple, and adorned the city with various edifices. But in A.D. 70 the Jews rebelled against Titus. The Romans then laid siege to the city and destroyed it.

In modern history Jerusalem has been ruled by Arabs, Turks, Christians, Germans, Egyptians, and finally the British. In 1948 the city was divided between the Jews and Arabs and stayed that way until the Six-Day War in June 1967. Then the city came entirely under the control of the Jews and nation of Israel. Politically it's still so, although the city is divided into religious sectors.

When the Book of Revelation talks about the New Jerusalem, what does it mean? Revelation 3:12 tells us it is the name of the city of our God and will come down out of heaven from God. Revelation 21 describes the new heaven, the new earth, and the New Jerusalem in detail. Turn to that passage now, and read about the incredible dwelling place God has planned for His people.

The point is that from ancient history to postmodern history, the Holy City plays a starring role in God's plan. We are beginning in Revelation 11 to get a glimpse of Jerusalem's later role as John is told to measure the temple, and then we are introduced to the two witnesses. Verse 8 points out that it was the city where Christ was crucified and that evil has reigned there from time to time. The reference to Sodom indicates moral degradation, divine judgment, and rejection of God's servants. In Isaiah 1:10 rebellious leaders of Jerusalem were called *rulers of Sodom.* Sodom represents vice and evil. Egypt represents vanity and enslavement of Israel. It was the country out of which Israel was delivered.

So there is prophecy yet to be fulfilled in the Holy City. Revelation 11 tells us that the city will be taken over by godless Gentile nations for three and a half years. That means the Jews will not be in control of Jerusalem at that time. Also, the two witnesses will reside in the City of David. Undoubtedly the whole world will view them as they testify. Through God's power they protect themselves from evil, are overcome and killed by the beast, and then

are resurrected after three and a half days. Finally, chapter 11 tells us there will be a tremendous earthquake that will destroy one-tenth of the city and cause 7,000 fatalities. This doesn't touch on other prophecies regarding Jerusalem in the end times. Stay tuned—there's lots of action yet to come in the Holy City.

David told us in 1 Chronicles 23:25, *He [God] dwells in Jerusalem forever.* We are admonished in the Psalms to pray for the peace of Jerusalem. Psalm 122:6 tells us, *Pray for the peace of Jerusalem: "May they prosper who love you."*

So the Holy City represents the presence of God and peace, but also promise. Evil, along with righteousness, has always been a part of Jerusalem's history. But one day that will all be put aside, and the New Jerusalem will be holy and pure and filled with the glory of God. The Holy City will be pure gold and like clear glass, adorned with every kind of precious stone. The place will need no temple, sun, or moon, for the Lamb will be these. Nothing unclean will be there, but only those whose names are written in the Lamb's book of life. We are promised that one day Jerusalem will truly be a Holy City (Revelation 21:10). If our names are written in the book, we are promised residency (verse 27). Hallelujah!

DAY TWO

The Temple

Read Revelation 11:1-2, 19.

1. In Revelation 11:1-2, John was told to measure what three things? What was he told not to measure?

2. Briefly summarize other times when people in the Bible were told to measure.

   Ezekiel 40:5

   Zechariah 2:1-2

   Revelation 21:15

3. What do you think the purposes of measuring might be? Summarize the following.

   Jeremiah 13:25

   2 Corinthians 10:13

4. The Temple in Scripture has three meanings. Fill in the meaning for each by looking up the passages.

   _____ Matthew 21:12
   Luke 2:46

   _____ 1 Corinthians 3:16
   1 Corinthians 6:19

   _____ Ephesians 2:18-21
   1 Peter 2:4-5

5. How long is 42 months in years? What significance does this number have? Summarize Daniel 7:25 and 12:6-7 (time = one year).

6. What does Revelation 11:19 mean? Refer to the reading of Revelation 21 from yesterday's lesson if necessary.

Do you realize that John had the vision of Revelation 20 years after Jerusalem and the Temple were destroyed? Now in the first verses of Revelation 11, he is told to measure the Temple, the altar, and those who worship in the Temple. How could he do this? The measuring had a purpose. Measuring is a symbol of the ownership of God.

The Temple and altar are not difficult to understand as far as what was to be measured. But how was John to measure those who worship in the Temple? Most commentators believe this means he was to measure the Church of Jesus Christ. It's believed to be a prelude to the sealing of the 144,000, which is an exact measurement. Are these 144,000 converted Jews who then become witnesses like the two witnesses? Certainly in Revelation 7 we are told that there are 12,000 from each tribe. This represents a sealing or the protection of God's people. "Temple" in Scripture represents God's people in some passages. Be aware that in other scriptures it may represent the actual physical structure of the Temple and also our physical bodies as believers.

Because John is told to measure the Temple, we know that when the end times come there will have to be a Temple. Are you aware that the Jewish people, God's chosen people, don't have a Temple now? There's to be only one Temple, and on a specific site in Jerusalem. Due to the disobedience of God's people, their city and Temple were destroyed in A.D. 70. The Jews did not even have their own nation again after that time until 1949. Can you grasp the full impact of a people going more than 1,800 years without their own country and then resurfacing and gaining enough political power to again be a nation? That would be like the United States being overrun, but generation after generation keeping hope alive of a new nation, and in A.D. 3878 a new government of the United States being established. What a miracle!

Another miracle is needed with regard to the Temple. For years the Jews have laid plans to rebuild their Temple, but one large obstacle has stood in their way: the Dome of the Rock, the third most important site of the Islamic faith. Jews and Christians are not allowed to worship here—only Muslims. But if the Temple has to be rebuilt on this site, how will it be possible with the Dome of the Rock there? In the last 10 years a Jewish engineer has done an exhaustive study in trying to pinpoint the exact location of the

Temple. He actually has come up with a spot north of the Dome of the Rock that's a relatively clear area, basically occupied only by a small shrine called the Dome of the Spirits. Many who have looked at his calculations believe him to be correct, giving hope for the first time of the possibility of rebuilding the Temple soon. To have the privilege of watching God perform miracles to work out His prophecies is exciting. As we study, let's pay attention and allow God to give us insight. We can have a front-row seat!

Revelation 11 concludes with showing us the ark of the covenant in the temple of God in heaven. Just as we studied yesterday that the Holy City is a promise for us, so we again see that God protects and preserves His promises for us. Although the ark of the covenant is lost to the inhabitants of this modern world, it is safely preserved by God in heaven along with all of His promises to us. One day we will reside there, where not only the temple is, but all things, including the ark, will be perfect as God planned them.

MEMORY CHALLENGE

How great is God's loving-kindness to those who fear Him?

DAY THREE

Two Witnesses

Read Revelation 11:3-6.

1. According to verse 4, who are the two witnesses?

2. How does Zechariah 4:12-14 further describe them?

3. What do each of the following represent in Scripture? (Hint: you will get many answers. Is there a way they all fit together?)

   Olive trees
       Exodus 27:20

       Psalm 52:8

       Jeremiah 11:16

       Romans 11:17, 24

   Lampstands
       Exodus 35:14

       Revelation 1:20

4. God grants the two witnesses authority and gives them power over what three things (verse 6)?

5. While there is not total agreement, most commentators think these two men are Moses and Elijah. Record the miracle performed by each next to the scripture.

   Exodus 7:14-17

   1 Kings 17:1

   2 Kings 1:10-12

6. What do you think the purposes of the two witnesses might be?

7. Do you believe God ever grants such authority and power to a Christian today? Why or why not? Back up your answer with scriptures if possible.

One of the most fascinating aspects of the Book of Revelation is the two witnesses. Jerry Jenkins and Tim LaHaye have written a series of novels about the Rapture and Tribulation. In their concept, these two witnesses are modern-day Jews dressed in sackcloth, representing Moses and Elijah. They stay in an area of Jerusalem surrounded by a chain-link fence where crowds come to gape at them as if they're animals in a zoo. The men prophesy, sometimes together and often taking turns. Other times they rest, but the message is always the same—about Christ and that He is the Messiah. They proclaim that people need to repent and accept Him as their Savior, that judgment is coming. When someone approaches to harm them, they simply breathe fire out of their mouths and, by doing so, consume the person or even an entire army. They perform miracles, calling down drought, death, and disease. No one can harm them until their testimony is complete and God allows it.[1]

Deuteronomy 19:15 tells us that in Judaic law at least two witnesses are required in court. Jesus affirmed this in Matthew 18:16 when He instructed that a brother in sin who would not listen needed to be confronted by two or three believers. In Mark 9, when Jesus was transfigured before the eyes of Peter, James, and John, two appeared to them along with Jesus. They were Elijah and Moses. Christ sent His disciples out in pairs in Mark 6:7. When Jesus needed a colt to ride into Jerusalem on what became Palm Sunday, He sent two disciples to get it (Matthew 21:1-2).

When God instructed Moses to go to Pharaoh to ask him to let His people go, Moses asked for a helper. He got Aaron. When Moses sent the spies into the Promised Land to determine whether the people could overrun the inhabitants and become the landowners, two spies, Joshua and Caleb, stood together so that the Hebrews could overcome. God created marriage for two to be together. Christ promised us that *where two or three have gathered together in My name, I am there in their midst* (Matthew 18:20).

Of all the amazing powers the two witnesses have, it is still striking that there are two. God could have given power to just one. But so often He gives us a partner. Just as He created us so He could have fellowship, God knows we need fellowship and often are stronger with another.

Socially we tend to pair off. Financially, many families have two incomes. Often in jobs we are assigned to teams. But what about in spiritual matters? Do we tend to go it alone? Do we have a spiritual mentor or partner? There is power in two or more. *Two are better than one because they have a good return for their labor. For if either of them falls, the one will lift up his companion. But woe to the one who falls when there is not another to lift him up* (Ecclesiastes 4:9-10).

The olive tree and lampstand need each other. In Scripture the olive tree represents Israel, the righteous, the Gentile believers, and the Church. But the necessity of providing oil for lamps is also seen. The lampstands provide light and need oil in order to do so (Exodus 35:14), but Revelation 1:20 also tells us the lampstands represent the churches. In a sense the olive trees and lampstands could be interpreted to mean the same thing. But note that they could not work out their function without the other. A lampstand is no good without oil to fuel it. Oil to provide light is useless without a lampstand. The two each need the other in order to function and be productive.

In December 1932 a woman touched by A. J. Russell's *For Sinners Only* asked a godly friend to sit down with her every day with pen and paper in hand to try and listen to what God may tell them. When she had attempted this alone, she received no guidance. But with this deeply spiritual friend she gained beautiful messages at every sitting. Soon she realized that they were being led and taught by the God of the universe himself. The lessons were never in conflict with God's Word and never failed them. Instead, they were powerful insights that encouraged, reproved, and refreshed.

These messages were eventually published in a devotional format by A. J. Russell as *God Calling*, giving many generations one of the most powerful daily readings available. As you read this classic, you get a feel for the power in two as God instructs both to hold each other accountable while supporting and encouraging each other to live out the messages they receive. One person cannot hide or ignore the message, for it was given to both. They are both aware that they are caretakers of it. A race is easier to run with two people. One pushes the other. A spiritual journey is easier to walk with another.

Who is your spiritual partner? Do you have two or more to encourage, enlighten, empower? We really do need each other. God did not send only one witness. He sent two. If you do not have another, pray that He will lead you to someone to make two.

MEMORY CHALLENGE

On a separate sheet of paper, write the memory verse several times.

DAY FOUR

Time for Evil

Read Revelation 11:7-10.

1. Who will overcome the two witnesses, and what will happen to the witnesses afterward?

2. Who is this beast? Read the following scriptures and summarize the portions regarding the beast.

   Daniel 7:19-21 (primarily summarize verse 21)

   Revelation 13:1-10 (summarize verse 7)

   Revelation 17:8

3. What is one of the great indignities to a Jew in his or her culture? See 1 Kings 13:22 and Psalm 79:3.

4. How will those who dwell on the earth respond to the death of the two witnesses?

5. In our society, when do we rejoice by giving gifts to each other?

John had seen and recorded from his vision terrible destruction, judgment, and sorrow. But now two lampstands appear for the Lord, bringing a little light to the world. The light was quickly snuffed out, sealing the power of the beast. Instead of the world viewing the two witnesses as good and the beast as evil for killing them, the world hated the light of the witnesses. *This is the judgment, that the Light has come into the world, and men loved the darkness rather than the Light, for their deeds were evil* (John 3:19).

Israel had times in its history when people became very evil, and it seemed as if no one was following God. When Elijah was prophesying to King Ahab, he felt as though he were standing alone. 1 Kings 18:22 states, *Then Elijah said to the people, "I alone am left a prophet of the LORD, but Baal's prophets are 450 men."*

We have seen this in modern history, as in World War II when Adolf Hitler of Germany had thousands of Jews executed simply because they were Jews. But think of a time in the world when possibly all the Christians are gone. Who would stand up for what's right or challenge the world to be moral? When an atrocity occurred, who would come forward to correct it? Who would be light to a dark and evil world?

The two witnesses will be served a great injustice when no one will take pity on them and bury their bodies. Even Joseph of Arimathea came forward to bury Jesus. But in full view of the world, probably due to television, these men lie there dead. No decency, no one with light is left on earth to show respect to the bodies and properly care for them.

Instead, the beast is made to look like the good guy because of his murder of the two witnesses. The evil world does not recognize that this is only because God allows it. They are thrilled and therefore celebrate. Christians in today's society give each other gifts at Christmas in remembrance of the gift God gave us of His Son. But when the two witnesses are killed, presents will be exchanged to commemorate an evil happening. There's no doubt—evil will reign for a time.

In the Bible, good and evil are always contrasted. They are opposites. Total evil wipes out good; total good will eliminate all evil. The passage studied today represents the time of evil allowed by the Orchestrator of the universe. Thank God—it's not the end of the story! Tomorrow we will see God's power and glory.

MEMORY CHALLENGE

Another term for "good" is "loving-kindness." Read Psalm 36 and relate how it and this week's memory challenge contrast good and evil.

DAY FIVE

Triumph and Terror

Read Revelation 11:11-14.

1. What happened to the dead bodies of the two witnesses after three and a half days?

2. Had this ever happened on earth before? Summarize the following scriptures.

   2 Kings 2:11

   Matthew 28:5-8

   Mark 5:35-43

3. For insight into the power of God over life and death, summarize one of the most fascinating stories of the Old Testament. The Valley of the Dry Bones is found in Ezekiel 37:1-10.

4. What happens next after the two witnesses are called into heaven?

5. What was the reaction of the people in Jerusalem first to this resurrection of two dead bodies and then to the mighty earthquake?

6. Why do you believe Jesus' entry into Jerusalem on Palm Sunday has become known as "the Triumphal Entry"?

Remarkable events elicit strong feelings. In the New Testament certain phrases are used referring to the miracles of Jesus: *Trembling and astonishment had gripped them* (Mark 16:8); *They were all amazed and were glorifying God, saying, "We have never seen anything like this"*

(2:12); *All the people . . . asked Him to leave them, for they were gripped with great fear* (Luke 8:37). Imagine being present in the Valley of Dry Bones when God began to put parts back together, connecting sinews, making flesh grow back over them, adding skin. Then breath came into the bones, and they came to life—incredible!

This kind of power can be very frightening or moving. Have you ever huddled in the bathtub of a house fearing the power of a tornado hovering overhead? Have you ever been blasted by a powerful wave as you tried to surf it? Have you ever been gathered with a body of believers when the Holy Spirit came in power and someone began to shout? Have you ever witnessed a miracle of God like a healing? Do any of these events leave your emotions untouched? Not unless you have so stifled your emotions that they are no longer a part of your being. These kinds of events inevitably bring strong reactions.

A believer in Jerusalem on this day of triumph and terror would experience a variety of emotions, but fear would be one of focus. The power of being able to resurrect two dead men would be so foreign that fear would be a natural response. An earthquake killing 7,000 people would also be cause for alarm. (It is interesting to note that the largest fault line in the world runs under Jerusalem.) So certainly anyone in the Holy City on this day would be afraid.

Yet the believer would have quiet confidence that God was in control, for He foretold all these events. Christians will not be surprised by the events. But imagine being an unbeliever and having no idea what in the world is going on! You would no doubt be terrified. If you didn't have knowledge of a God with the power to raise the dead, seeing these two dead men rise would be astonishing. Before your emotions could process that event, the earthquake would begin, and you would be even more frightened.

Because we have been given the Word of God and the Book of Revelation, we have a choice about how the end times affect us. Yes, even believers will be afraid. But it should not be an uncontrollable terror, because we know the end of the story. For the believers will be triumphant, as when Jesus was hailed King on Palm Sunday and when He arose from the grave.

John Phillips in *Exploring Revelation* states that this passage shows judgment on earth and jubilation in heaven. It displays rage on earth and rejoicing in heaven; cursing on earth and crowning in heaven. Finally, he points out that it reveals woe on earth and worship in heaven. There will be contrast for the believers and unbelievers.[1] We choose how it will be for us now. That day will be triumphant or full of terror. Which will you choose?

MEMORY CHALLENGE

What does it mean to fear Him? Is this the same type of terror talked about in the lesson today?

DAY SIX

Thy Kingdom Come

Read Revelation 11:15-19.

1. What did the loud voices in heaven say when the seventh angel sounded its trumpet?

2. Record Matthew 6:10.

3. The 24 elders worship God in verse 17. Compare it to Revelation 1:8, and record which phrase is missing.

4. Read Revelation 11:18-19, and explain why the above phrase is missing.

5. What do you think the kingdom of heaven is like? Give ideas from the following verses.

   Mark 12:32-34

   Luke 1:33

   Luke 17:20-21

   Luke 23:42-43

   1 Corinthians 4:20

   Hebrews 12:28

6. What do we mean when we pray as part of the Lord's Prayer, *Thy kingdom come. Thy will be done in earth, as it is in heaven* (Matthew 6:10, KJV)?

In the height of the Chicago Bulls' NBA reign of the 1990s, they were an unbelievably powerful team. When they played one of the poorer teams of the league, they were sure to win. But if the Bulls played their best for the entire game, they would win by a huge margin. Instead, for the first three quarters they would play just hard enough to stay ahead. However, when the fourth quarter arrived, they would spring into top form. The game would conclude in an easy win for the Bulls. They didn't need to strain and exhaust themselves the whole game. They were so powerful that the fourth quarter was all it took.

When we come to the end of Revelation 11, we get the same sense. God has been in control of the situation all along and was allowing a time for evil to reign. But now it is the last hour, and He begins to unleash His power. It's no contest. He will now accomplish His will.

The kingdoms of the earth have belonged to Satan up until this time. He told Jesus in Luke 4:6, *I will give You all this domain and its glory; for it has been handed over to me, and I give it to whomever I wish.* Notice that Satan admitted that they had been given to him. Who was the original owner? *For God is the King of all the earth* (Psalm 47:7). *The Most High God is ruler over the realm of mankind and . . . He sets over it whomever He wishes* (Daniel 5:21). The kingdoms of earth are God's, but in His permissive will He allowed humanity free choice, and therefore Satan reigned on earth for a time.

Christ did not want the kingdoms of the earth until they were going to be the kingdom of heaven on earth. The pure Prince could reign only over holiness. But the time has now come, so in verse 17 we see that the phrase *who is to come* is left out, for the time is now here—Christ will begin His reign on earth.

Christ told us so much about His kingdom while He was on earth. Sixty-nine times He referred to the kingdom of God in some form or fashion. He tells us what heaven is like and that God's plan is for that type of kingdom to reign on earth. Christ explains what we will be like in His kingdom and how His kingdom reigns in us as we do the Father's will. Until Revelation 11 is accomplished, we as believers are God's kingdom on earth. When we pray *Thy kingdom come. Thy will be done in earth, as it is in heaven* (Matthew 6:10, KJV), we pray for Revelation 11 to be fulfilled, but we also pray for ourselves, that we will live according to Kingdom principles. What a promise and challenge! We are promised the Kingdom, but we are challenged to live like Kingdom people now, bringing God's kingdom to earth. May we make *Thy kingdom come* our prayer and lifestyle.

Written by Linda Shaw

MEMORY CHALLENGE

Recite this week's memory verse aloud.

Notes

Introduction to Revelation
1. *Expositor's Bible Commentary* (Grand Rapids: Zondervan Publishing House, 1981), 12:399.
2. William Barclay, *The Daily Study Bible Series: The Revelation of John*, rev. ed. (Philadelphia: Westminster Press, 1976), 1:20.

Lesson 1, Day 2
1. John Phillips, *Exploring Revelation* (Chicago: Moody Press, 1987), 19.

Lesson 1, Day 3
1. Ibid., 23-24.

Lesson 1, Day 4
1. Quoted in Richard J. Foster, *Celebration of Discipline* (New York: Harper & Row, 1978), 149.

Lesson 1, Day 6
1. Henry T. Blackaby and Claude V. King, *Experiencing God: Knowing and Doing the Will of God* (Nashville: Lifeway Press, 1973), 184.

Lesson 3, Day 1
1. Barclay, *Daily Study Bible Series: Revelation*, n.p.

Lesson 3, Day 2
1. *The Revelation of St. John the Divine*, vol. 5 of *Expositor's Greek Testament* (Grand Rapids: Wm. B. Eerdmans Publishing Co., n.d.), 364.

Lesson 3, Day 3
1. *The Reader's Digest Great Encyclopedic Dictionary* (Pleasantville, N.Y.: The Reader's Digest Association, 1966), 1437.
2. Barclay, *Daily Study Bible Series: Revelation*, 127.

Lesson 3, Day 6
1. Ibid., 146.

Lesson 4, Day 1
1. Paraphrased from Paul Marshall, *Their Blood Cries Out: The Untold Story of Persecuted Christians in the Modern World* (Dallas: Word Books, 1997), 149.
2. From a letter dated August 2, 1995, in ibid., 151.

Lesson 4, Day 2
1. Billy Graham, syndicated column, Tribune Media Services, n.d.

Lesson 4, Day 4
1. This material is taken from "God's Final Word," by Ray C. Stedman. Copyright 1991 by Ray C. Stedman. Used by permission of Discovery House Publishers, Box 3566, Grand Rapids, MI 49501.

Lesson 4, Day 5
1. Ibid.

Lesson 5, Day 3
1. *Guideposts Family Concordance* (Nashville: Thomas Nelson Publishers, 1982), 338.

Lesson 6, Day 2
1. This material is taken from "God's Final Word," by Ray C. Stedman. Copyright 1991 by Ray C. Stedman. Used by permission of Discovery House Publishers, Box 3566, Grand Rapids, MI 49501.

Lesson 6, Day 3
1. Ibid.

Lesson 6, Day 4
1. From a news story in the *Oklahoma City Sunday Oklahoman*, August 9, 1998.

Lesson 7, Day 4
1. *Life Application Study Bible* (Wheaton, Ill.: Tyndale House Publishers, 1988), s.v. Romans 3.
2. Ibid., s.v. Rom. 3:23.

Lesson 7, Day 5
1. Thomas R. Kelly, *A Testament of Devotion* (New York: Harper & Row, 1941), 39.
2. Brother Lawrence, *The Practice of the Presence of God* (Old Tappan, N.J.: Fleming H. Revell Co., 1958), 43.

Lesson 8, Day 1
1. Earl F. Palmer, *Mastering the New Testament* (Nashville: Thomas Nelson Publishers, 1979), 185.
2. This material is taken from "God's Final Word," by Ray C. Stedman. Copyright 1991 by Ray C. Stedman. Used by permission of Discovery House Publishers, Box 3566, Grand Rapids, MI 49501.
3. Ibid.

Lesson 8, Day 2
1. David A. Ridenour, "Vice President Carries Own Baggage," *Oklahoma City Daily Oklahoman*, September 7, 1998, 6A.

Lesson 8, Day 5
1. This material is taken from "God's Final Word," by Ray C. Stedman. Copyright 1991 by Ray C. Stedman. Used by permission of Discovery House Publishers, Box 3566, Grand Rapids, MI 49501.

Lesson 9, Day 2
1. Barclay, *Daily Study Bible Series: Revelation*, 2:49-50.
2. Ralph Earle, *Revelation*, vol. 10 of *Beacon Bible Commentary* (Kansas City: Beacon Hill Press of Kansas City, 1967), 556.

Lesson 9, Day 4
1. Josh McDowell and Don Stewart, *Answers to Tough Questions: Skeptics Ask About the Christian Faith* (San Bernardino, Calif.: Here's Life Publishers, 1980), 154.

Lesson 9, Day 5
1. J. Vernon McGee, *Revelation* (chapters 6—13), vol. 59 of *Through the Bible Commentary Series* (Nashville: Thomas Nelson Publishers, 1991), 109.

Lesson 10, Day 5
1. William Barclay, *John, Jude, and Revelation* (Glasgow: St. Andrew Press, 1960), 69.

Lesson 10, Day 6
1. Quoted in Earle, *Revelation*, 561.

Lesson 11, Day 3
1. Tim LaHaye and Jerry Jenkins, *Left Behind* (Wheaton, Ill.: Tyndale House Publishers, 1995), 301.

Lesson 11, Day 5
1. Phillips, *Exploring Revelation*, 151.